Supply-Chain Survival in the Age of Globalization

Supply-Chain Survival in the Age of Globalization

By James A. Pope

First published in 2011 by
Business Expert Press, LLC
222 East 46th Street, New York, NY 10017
www.businessexpertpress.com

ISBN-13: 978-160649-163-8

ISBN-13: 978-160649-164-5

DOI 10.4128/ 9781606491645

A publication in the Business Expert Press Supply and Operations
Management collection

Collection ISSN: 2156-8189
Collection ISSN: 2156-8200

Cover design by Jonathan Pennell
Interior design by Scribe Inc.

First edition: September 2011

10 9 8 7 6 5 4 3 2 1

Printed in the United States of America.

*To my wife, Sally Coulter, whose support
and editing made this a far better book*

Abstract

When supply-chain management moves into the global arena the problems are profoundly different from those in domestic supply chains. This book will examine the history and background of global supply chains, some of the unique problems faced when managing a global supply chain, and some ways of dealing with these problems. Each chapter ends with suggested action items for the global supply-chain manager.

Keywords

Chain master, China, culture, ethics, global, globalization, insourcing, JIT, international, lean, logistics, operations management, outsourcing, risk management, security, supply-chain management, trade, transportation.

Contents

About the Author

James A. Pope

Professor Pope is a guest professor at the Baden-Würtemburg Cooperative State University in Mosbach, Germany. Over a 45-year career—40 in academia and 5 as a U.S. Air Force logistics officer—he held full-time academic positions at Guilford College in North Carolina, Old Dominion University in Virginia, Shippensburg University of Pennsylvania, the European Business School in Germany, and the University of Toledo in Ohio. He has also been a guest at the University of Colorado in Denver; the University of North Carolina; North Carolina A&T University; the Technical University of Munich; Leiden University in the Netherlands; the University of Regensburg in Germany; and PSGIM in Coimbatore, India. He holds a PhD in business administration from the University of North Carolina and degrees in economics from Northwestern University and the College of Wooster in Ohio. He has done consulting and writing in a variety of operations areas, including inventory management, logistics, scheduling, quality, and supply chain management. Dr. Pope is the coauthor of *Ocean Container Transportation: An Operational Perspective*. He is APICS certified (CFPIM and CSCP) and has taught APICS certification review courses for 30 years. He can be found on LinkedIn and Xing.

Acknowledgments

The staffs at Business Expert Press and Scribe made the technical aspects of writing this book easy. My reviewers—Dick Crandall, Ram Rachamadugu, and Bruce Brechin—provided valuable insights and suggestions. My colleagues, both academic and practitioner, and my students over the years were a major source of my accumulated knowledge in the subject of global supply-chain management.

Foreword

Although supply-chain management as a concept is moving into its third decade, there is still much to learn and a multitude of challenges to overcome. Starting from early problems such as software communication, to maintaining quality throughout the supply chain, to overcoming the bullwhip effect, globalization is at the heart of many of the current challenges in managing supply chains. Globalization has stretched supply chains, introduced a variety of problems not present in purely domestic supply chains, and raised serious issues of security and economic survival.

Many firms have treated global supply chains as if they were a simple extension of the domestic model. This has caused unexpected problems, including hidden costs, quality problems, the difficulty of managing supply chains on a global basis, and a general backlash against outsourcing. Western industry learned some hard lessons about just-in-time (JIT) and lean processes in the 1980s when it was unprepared for Japanese competition. About the time businesses were learning the lessons, the rules changed again with the introduction of supply-chain management concepts and the rapid growth of globalization.

This book will trace the history of these developments—looking at the things that were done right and should have been done better and examining the problems and some of the solutions for global supply chains in today's world. Western industry faced a significant challenge from the Japanese in the 1980s and managed to fight back (largely successfully). The current challenge is to succeed in the face of global competition. Good supply-chain management is necessary and critical for winning this competition.

CHAPTER 1

Background

Supply chains have existed ever since humans began trading with other tribes. Archaeologists have found evidence of artifacts far from where they are known to have originated. In historic times, the civilizations around the Mediterranean were active traders and even ventured outside the Mediterranean to the west coast of Africa to look for items they wanted. The Byzantines, in the seventh century AD, developed interchangeable parts manufacturing and a supply chain involving the church and the army to support their wars against the Persian Empire.[1] Marco Polo established a global supply chain with Asian countries. From the 15th century onward, the nations of Europe established trade routes and global supply chains from America, India, the East Indies, and Africa. Some of these supply chains brought products that had been previously scarce or unknown in Europe, such as spices, rubber, tobacco, and cotton. Around 1850, an important industry in Baltimore, Maryland, was the manufacture of haircloth for covering furniture. The hair component in the cloth was horsehair from Siberia.[2] Global supply chains stretched around the world. Some supply chains brought shame, such as those transporting slaves to the Americas and Arabia. More recently, there has been a growth in global supply chains in illegal drugs, human trafficking, and banned substances such as ivory.

A big difference between merchants of old and today was the risks they took. Traders of yore had no GPS or satellite tracking systems, no e-mail, no telex, and no telephone or telegraph of any kind. The expression "when my ship comes in" stems from investors in ventures to the far-flung ends of the supply chains—stretching as far as India or the East Indies—waiting to see if their investments would pay off. They literally had to wait until the ship arrived many months or even years after embarking with no word from it in the interim.

Much of this current growth in global trade may be attributed to technological advances. Improvements in transportation, especially the introduction of containerization by Malcolm McLean in 1955,[3] reduced the "transportation cost" barrier to trade and speeded the movement of goods. Communication improved dramatically starting with the first wireless transmissions by Guglielmo Marconi in 1895. Deregulation made it easier to trade, and the development of institutions to facilitate transactions and the increasing sophistication of the banking system all contributed to the expansion of global trade. Governments began to recognize the importance of trade, and trade barriers were lowered, especially after World War II. The theoretical nature of the economics of this reduction in transaction costs is described in Oliver Williamson's Nobel Prize–winning work.[4]

Supply Chain Issues: Old and New

Some of today's burning issues are similar or identical to those of 100 or more years ago. In 1771, Richard Arkwright built a mill in Cromford, England, which gave the English a competitive advantage in the manufacture of textiles. The English were serious about protecting their intellectual property; the penalty for attempting to leave the country with a copy of the plans was hanging! Samuel Slater built an Arkwright mill in the United States in 1791 by memorizing the plans and sailing to America, thereby starting the Industrial Revolution in North America.[5] Throughout the first part of the 19th century, England depended on the American South to supply its mills with cotton. The issue of cotton became important during the American Civil War when there was a lot of debate in England over which side to support.[6] Because of the Union blockade of Confederate ports, the price of cotton in London reached heights it would not reach again until 2010.[7] Management of supply chains was important for both sides in the U.S. Civil War. Coffee for the troops, for example, was an important import for the Union army; the army would buy only whole coffee beans to prevent the vendors from "stretching" the coffee by adding sawdust or other contaminants. This was a clear case of lack of trust in the supply chain, and they devised a method to insure the security of the product (in other words, to insure that they got what they ordered).

The Theoretical Grounds for Globalization

The theoretical grounds for global supply chains were laid by Adam Smith in 1776 with the publication of his *An Inquiry into the Nature and Causes of the Wealth of Nations*. Prior to Smith, the mercantilist school of thought argued that a nation's wealth was the amount of gold it had accumulated. Smith argued that wealth was the goods and services available for consumption. His argument for free trade and specialization (in his story of division of labor among the pin makers)[8] eventually provided support for the repeal of the "corn laws" in England (basically, reducing the tariffs on agricultural goods). His theory of absolute advantage and David Ricardo's theory of comparative advantage argued that nations should specialize in what they do best relative to other nations.[9] This is essentially what globalization is all about.

The Scope of Globalization

Globalization today, of course, is on a much larger scale than it was over 100 years ago, and there are many more players—both firms and countries. In fact, the word "globalization" was scarcely used before the 1990s. The *Economist* reported that "the word seldom appeared" in its pages "before 1986, and began to be common only in the 1990s."[10] A classic example of the modern development of the global economy was the bidding for Arcelor, the steel firm based in Luxembourg. The two bidders were from Brazil and India. Twenty or even 10 years ago, both of these countries were considered to be underdeveloped, and neither would have had players in the bidding. Closer to home in the United States, the three largest U.S. brewers of beer are now owned by non-U.S. firms. Miller Brewing Company was purchased by a South African firm in 2002, Coors Brewing Company by Canadians in 2005, and Anheuser-Busch by Belgians in 2008.

Sometimes the links in the global supply chain are not as stable as one would like. In fact, most of the time the average person is unaware of the links and how events around the globe can have a serious impact on business around the world. Bolivia, for example, has the world's largest reserves of lithium, a critical material in batteries for powering everything from our mobile phones to the new electric automobiles. Bolivia has been going through a lot of political turmoil. The Democratic Republic of the Congo, where revolution and fighting seem to be constant, is the world's leading supplier of cobalt, a vital component in jet aircraft engines.[11] It is also a leading supplier of tantalum, which is used in smartphones.[12] There are many other examples—from rare earth in China to platinum in Zimbabwe (not to mention Middle East petroleum)—of how vital links in the global supply chain can become embroiled in political maneuverings. Even the U.S. Congress has gotten involved. The 2010 Dodd-Frank financial-regulation law identified four minerals mined in the Congo that are used to generate funds for violent conflict there. Companies are required to report to the Securities and Exchange Commission (SEC) "whether any of [the four minerals] in their supply chains originated in the Congo or nine neighboring countries."[13]

In the 1950s, trade with other countries was so insignificant in the United States—about 5% of the gross national product (GNP)—that the government did not even measure GDP (gross domestic product) separately from GNP.[14] The difference was trade, which was negligible. Today, trade is about 24% of our GDP. Global trade has become a significant part of America's economic life.

Vertical Integration

As U.S. industrialization moved ahead rapidly in the last part of the 19th century, the competition among the industrialists was fierce. Personalities with large egos, such as Vanderbilt, Gould, Rockefeller, and Carnegie, dominated the economic scene. Partially because of these rivalries, the issue of securing dependable sources of supply became important. The answer to securing these sources was what is known today as vertical integration. Vertical integration was the incorporation of much or all of the supply chain into one company. The master of this approach was Henry Ford. Not only did he refine the modern discrete production line, but he vertically integrated his supply chain from the sources of iron ore to his steel mills, to his fabrication and assembly operations in his River Rouge plant, to the dealerships that sold his cars.

Vertical integration ebbs and flows like a fad. Firms will move away from vertical integration with the rationalization that they should concentrate on their "core competencies." Then, as they run into problems, they move in the other direction. Boeing's strategy for the development and production of its 787 Dreamliner jet aircraft has been to outsource much of the design and production of components, with the final assembly taking place in Seattle, Washington. The major structural parts of the aircraft are produced in nine different countries. Because of recurring quality problems in the fuselage assembly, Boeing decided to purchase a factory from a major supplier, Vought Aircraft Industries,[15] to get more control over the quality—in other words, a partial vertical reintegration. The Chinese are investing in raw materials such as coal in Australia[16] and oil in Africa to insure a steady flow of these commodities. Apple is "insourcing" some of its design functions from Asia to protect its intellectual property.[17] The steel maker ArcelorMittal has purchased iron ore mines to insure a steady flow of raw materials.

Summary

Supply chains have existed since humans began specializing and trading. Their rapid development in recent years has caused virtually everyone on the globe to be touched by them in some manner. At one point in his life, the author lived in a small town of 4,000 people in Pennsylvania. There were three supermarkets in the town. One was American, one was Belgian, and one was Dutch. Most of the residents were unaware of the international connections of two of the supermarkets, but they were in contact with their global supply chains virtually every day.

The supply-chain manager should keep a sense of perspective and remember the following:

- Global supply chains are not new; they are just more extensive and pervasive.
- There is a solid theoretical basis for global trade, supply chains, and outsourcing stretching back over 200 years.
- Identifying products or firms as being from one country or another may be a fruitless exercise. Even our "locally grown" food may have been raised using equipment made of parts produced in Thailand or India and using fuel refined from Saudi oil.

- There is no absolute rule about producing in-house or using an extensive chain of suppliers. Each situation is unique and must be assessed on its own merits.

CHAPTER 2

Post–World War II Developments

World War II turned out to be a major setback for American manufacturing. The country did learn a lot during the war about things such as design to production cycle reduction; quality control; learning curves; and operations research. Unfortunately, much of this knowledge was put aside after the war. The basic reason was that it was not needed. After the war, Japan and the industrialized nations of Europe were in ruins. The only significant production capability in the world was in the United States. Virtually everything the United States bought and used was made in the United States. Additionally, the United States supplied much of the rest of the world with manufactured goods. There was no competition. The focus in the auto industry, for example, was on design, not on quality. Tail fins sprouted and headlights multiplied. Even the Edsel was a well-designed car, but it failed partly because of multiple quality problems.

Symptomatic of the low expectation of quality during this era was the largest-selling imported car—the Volkswagen Beetle. Despite its relatively low price, it was considered a high-quality car with good fuel economy. In fact, it was cramped and noisy, had no cargo space, had the fuel tank in the front of the car, was almost impossible to heat in the winter, and was difficult to maintain. But it was made to tight specifications and felt "solid." It was even rumored to be so airtight that it would float. *Popular Science* magazine tested this rumor by dropping a Beetle in a pond. It did indeed float. Goods that did come from countries like Japan were considered to be cheap and of poor quality. One of the urban legends of the 1950s was that the Japanese changed the name of one of their cities to USA so that they could mark products made there as "Made in USA." The legend continued that American manufacturers marked their products "Made in U.S.A." to distinguish them from the Japanese products.

The Japanese were not idle, however. American quality gurus such as W. Edwards Deming and Joseph Juran were unable to generate interest in the United States in the 1950s, so they preached their message of quality control and total quality management to receptive audiences in Japan. Taiichi Ohno, the developer of the Toyota Production System (TPS), later known as just-in-time (JIT) or lean manufacturing, was an avid reader of Henry Ford's books on manufacturing. He is quoted as saying that if Henry Ford had lived longer, he would have developed the same system that Ohno did at Toyota.[1] He reportedly visited Detroit for ideas on how to produce cars. He was not impressed with what he saw in Detroit in the 1950s. What did impress him were U.S. supermarkets (supermarkets did not exist in Japan at the time). He observed the system for stocking shelves—replacing only what had been removed—and went home and used it as the basis for the pull production system using kanban (which allows restocking only when something has been used or removed from the inventory).

The Japanese "Invasion"

The impact of these efforts in Japan became visible when the first large-scale shipments of Japanese cars to the United States began in the late 1960s. Toyota, Nissan (then Datsun), Honda, and others began selling small, economical, well-made cars. They quickly penetrated the market because the competition, both American and German (Volkswagen), offered pathetic alternatives. The American business model was to make a basic car at the factory and ship it to the dealer. There, the customer chose from a list of options (at added cost), which the dealer installed. The dealer was referred to, half-jokingly, as the last station on the production line. The Japanese offered the options in a small number of factory-installed packages included in the already low price.

The Advent of APICS and MRP

Amid all this, there was virtually no progress or improvement in American production techniques from 1945 to 1975. After the Japanese wake-up call, the first major innovation in manufacturing came not from the manufacturers themselves but from advances in the computer world. The introduction of the IBM 370 brought computers to the point where they had enough processing power to be useful in the manufacturing sector. This computing power allowed the development of the system that began the transformation of U.S. manufacturing: material requirements planning (MRP), which based materials planning on anticipated needs rather than past experience. Joseph Orlicky, an employee of IBM, published the definitive book on MRP in 1975.[2]

In a parallel development, the production planners and material managers came together in 1958 to form the American Production and Inventory Management Society (APICS). They recognized the need for a common body of knowledge and the sharing of ideas. Men such as Oliver Wight, Orlicky, George Plossl, and Walter Goddard were instrumental in recognizing the need for new approaches to manufacturing and materials management in the United States. Prior to MRP, materials were managed using order point systems. Parts and raw materials for manufacturing were ordered in case they were needed. This led to inventories based on past usage rather than anticipated needs. These inventories tended to be large since one had to be prepared for an uncertain future.

MRP changed the approach to one that based inventory and materials management on the master schedule or the anticipated needs. Done correctly, this would mean that the only parts and raw materials in the inventory would be those needed to build the master schedule. This method could dramatically reduce the size and cost of inventories and smooth the production process, since parts and materials would always be available when (and only when) they were needed. The pioneering firms that first developed and used MRP in the early 1970s were J. I. Case, Twin Disc, Black & Decker, and PerkinElmer.[3] The advocates of MRP were so committed to it that they formed, through APICS, an MRP crusade to spread the word about its benefits to American manufacturers. They succeeded, and MRP became a core part of the APICS Body of Knowledge and the subject of one of its certification exams. Today, most manufacturing firms use some form of MRP or its derivatives (such as enterprise resource planning, or ERP).

JIT Comes to the United States

The Japanese were not sitting still, however. Ohno was at Toyota developing the TPS—later known as JIT. The United States learned of TPS when Kawasaki decided to introduce JIT into its motorcycle plant in Lincoln, Nebraska, in 1981. The company had just spent 4 years testing and refining JIT in its test plant in Japan and had decided to introduce it in all its plants worldwide.[4] Although JIT is a comprehensive system for reducing waste in the manufacturing process, in the United States it was initially perceived as a system for reducing inventories, especially work-in-process (WIP) inventories through the use of kanbans. This led to jokes among materials people such as, "JIT is a system for getting other people to carry your inventory for you." They missed the point that the inventory-control aspect was just one part of a total production management system. The concept of JIT was so different from the systems used in the United States at that time that the two biggest problems faced by Kawasaki were convincing their American managers to adopt the new system and integrating their suppliers into the system.

The most important contribution of JIT from a supply-chain point of view was the idea that a company should work with its suppliers and customers rather than treat them as the enemy. At the time, the common working assumption was that suppliers wanted to provide you with low quality at a high price and customers wanted high quality for a low price. In other words, it was an adversarial relationship. An example is a company in Suffolk, Virginia, that in the 1980s asked the author for advice on suing their customers in a court of law. The company's procedure was to accept an order, produce the order to the customer's specifications, and then check the customer's line of credit to see if there was sufficient credit to allow shipment. If not, the items were sent to the warehouse, where they waited until the customer made a payment on account. The customers learned that they could reach the limit on their lines of credit and still order items ahead of time. The items would then be ready and in the supplier's warehouse when they wanted them. Instead of changing the system to check the line of credit *before* starting production, or sitting down with the customers to reach a resolution, the company's reaction was to call the lawyers.

The JIT concept was considered so important that APICS began its second (and, to date, last) crusade in the early 1980s—the Zero Inventories Crusade. This also reflects the emphasis in the United States on the inventory-management aspects of JIT. Professor Robert Hall, an author who wrote about the Kawasaki case, wrote another book titled *Zero Inventories*.[5] There was a lot of debate in the 1980s over whether MRP or JIT was the most appropriate method for manufacturing management. One consultant stood up at an APICS conference and said, "MRP and JIT are like two fat men trying to get through a door at the same time. Only one can get through." He was a JIT consultant. Others felt that MRP could be used for planning and JIT for execution. JIT, like MRP before, was incorporated into the APICS Body of Knowledge and became the subject of one of its certification exams. Eventually the debate died down as manufacturing professionals realized (a) JIT was a total management philosophy and many of its ideas could be applied in any situation (including services) and (b) there were different ways to organize processes and each might require a different management method.

The Evolution of MRP and New Techniques

As computing power increased, MRP was extended to more and more areas in the firm, first becoming manufacturing resource planning (so-called closed-loop MRP II) and then ERP. The fundamental distinction is that ERP uses a single database for the entire enterprise, whether it is in one location or has multiple locations around the world. Some of its problems will be discussed in the next chapter.

Other Techniques

A number of other techniques were also developed to improve the production- and materials-management functions. In 1984, Eli Goldratt, an Israeli physicist, published his now-famous book *The Goal*.[6] It caused a bit of a sensation because it was written as a novel instead of an academic tome or a "how-to" book. It still appears from time to time on the bestseller lists of business books. In it, Goldratt applied the concept of bottleneck management. He initially incorporated his ideas in a software package named OPT (Optimized Production Technology), but he later sold the company and focused on education and training. He developed a certification known as "Jonah," named after the consultant who saved the day in *The Goal.* Goldratt codified his ideas into the theory of constraints (TOC) and extended his ideas to (and wrote books about) fields such as finance, marketing, and project management.

Although Goldratt wrote in the context of the individual firm, the concept of bottlenecks is just as important in supply chains. The 2011 earthquake and resulting tsunami in Japan exposed several bottlenecks that had not been widely known. Xirallic, for example—a component of paint for automobiles used by nearly all vehicle manufacturers—is made in just one factory in Japan. It was shut down by the earthquake.[7] Kureha, a Japanese firm, produces 70% of the world's supply of a critical polymer used in lithium batteries for mobile devices such as the iPhone. Their one factory was shut down by the same earthquake.[8] For the global electronics market, Japan makes 20% of the computer chips, 60% of the silicon wafers, and 90% of the BT resin used in circuit boards. All were curtailed by the earthquake.[9] Two companies in Korea, Samsung and Hynix, make about 60% of the global supply of computer chips.[10] The Anderson Development Company makes around 80% of the global supply of several acrylic resins at their Adrian, Michigan, facility. Although they do not have an earthquake or tsunami threat, the area is known for occasional violent storms and tornados. Anderson maintains redundant, separated capacity on the site as well as an off-site safety stock.[11] The consequences of bottlenecks in supply chains are just as important as in an individual facility, but they are far more difficult to identify and manage.

Other concepts for improving operations and supply-chain management that have been developed since the 1980s include sales and operations planning, value chain analysis, value engineering (analysis), Six Sigma, and quality function deployment. The field continues to develop rapidly.

Summary

There are many tools available to the supply-chain manager that did not exist 50 or even 20 years ago. It is important to be aware of these tools and to ensure that participants throughout the supply chain are aware of them and are trained in their use.

- Encourage (or even require) your employees to earn their certifications from APICS, the Institute for Supply Management (ISM), the Supply Chain Council, or other professional organizations.
- Create an atmosphere of innovation in process management.
- Know which of your suppliers are potential bottlenecks, and have a "plan B" in case they cannot meet your needs.
- Keep yourself and your colleagues current by attending professional meetings—locally, nationally, and internationally—where you can hear about the latest developments in supply-chain management and case studies of their application.

CHAPTER 3

The Supply-Chain Management Concept

Although supply chains have existed since prehistory when humans began to trade, the formal concept of supply-chain management is relatively new. As recently as January 1997, the APICS *Performance Advantage* issue had on its cover "Supply Chain Management: What Is It?" Reportedly, the first use of the term supply-chain management (SCM) was in a report in 1982 by consultants Oliver and Webber.[1] Once just-in-time (JIT) introduced the concept of working with one's immediate customers and suppliers, the extension in both directions to the entire supply chain was a logical concept. The transformation was not easy, as it was necessary to overcome decades of the materials-management concept, which basically considered the customers and suppliers to be the enemy.

Development of Supply-Chain Systems

The idea of managing a supply chain also raised technical problems. Much effort had been put into refining the MRP (material requirements planning)/ERP (enterprise resource planning) concept to make the internal workings of the firm ever more efficient. The late 1960s and early 1970s saw the development of MRP, which merged inventory planning with production planning. It was strictly internal to the firm. The only connections to outside firms were orders from customers and orders to vendors. MRP II added additional modules such as finance, accounting, and human resources but was still contained and operated within a single firm. Adding all internal resources to the MRP II system and merging all data into a single database yielded ERP—still an internal system. The parallel development of the lean systems philosophy in the 1980s meant that firms were beginning to consider supply chains of internal customers and suppliers. This functioned well in the MRP/ERP environment since the systems were still focused on the internal mechanisms of the firm. The integration of external customers and vendors into the supply chain, however, meant that supply chains were functioning as virtual companies—companies that were not legally a part of each other but operated as if they were. This new focus of SCM forced manufacturing and software firms to communicate more efficiently along the supply chain. Large firms might have hundreds of customers and thousands of suppliers with the resulting intertwined supply chains. AT&T estimates that the supply chain for its wireless handset includes "35 manufacturers, 60 to 80 parts suppliers, more than 1000 commodity-part suppliers, and an unknown number of brokers and distributors."[2] The technical difficulties in developing software and protocols to make the systems work together are daunting. In addition to the IT protocols, there are more mundane protocols that can cause problems. Should the measurement systems be British or metric? What are the stock-keeping units (SKUs)? In the United States, we often use multiples of 12, such as a dozen or a gross, but the rest of the world generally does not. Which nomenclature and language should be used? How does one assign item numbers to the inventory?

Development of the Body of Knowledge

One of the problems facing SCM professionals was the lack of a body of knowledge on SCM. Organizations such as APICS and the Purchasing Management Association (PMA) had defined bodies of knowledge in their areas that focused primarily on the individual firm. There was not even general agreement on an exact definition for a supply chain. The Supply Chain Council in 1996 was the first organization to develop a widely accepted definition and concept of a supply chain. They are an industry group composed of companies (as opposed to individuals) and initially conceived of supply-chain management as consisting of four processes: *planning* the entire chain; and, within each link, *sourcing* (either purchasing from outsiders or producing internally); *making* (the fabrication or assembly process at that stage in the chain); and *delivering* (to the customer, who could be anyone from the next workstation to the final customer). The chain (or, using their terminology, the "thread") itself would consist of five links: from the supplier's supplier, to the supplier, to the firm in question, to the customer, to the customer's customer.

A few years later they added *returning* as a fifth process to account for product returns because of poor quality, the wrong product shipped, the customer changing his or her mind, or recycling. For example, in the European Union (EU), automobiles are required to be 85% recyclable by weight. The manufacturers are responsible for taking back their cars and performing the recycling.[3] Clothing sellers often have a large number of returns based on customers changing their minds or incorrect sizing.

Their formulation was dubbed the Supply Chain Operational Reference Model, or SCOR. It has become the de facto standard definition of a supply chain. The SCOR model is more than just a fancy diagram, however. It is a multilayer modeling system for designing new supply chains and improving existing ones. Its three pillars are process modeling, performance measurement, and best practices. The Supply Chain Council offers extensive training in the use of their techniques.

Certification

In the early 2000s, the demand from professionals for certification in SCM knowledge led to APICS offering the certification exam, CSCP (Certified Supply Chain Professional), in 2006. The certification exam (in contrast to the CPIM [Certified in Production and Inventory Management] certification, which has five modules) consisted of one module with four parts:

- Understanding supply-chain management fundamentals
- Building a competitive infrastructure
- Managing customer and suppler relations
- Using information technology

The topics ranged from basic inventory and quality management to the Sarbanes-Oxley Act, to the technical details of data file management. Supply-chain certification has proven to be quite popular, so other organizations have introduced their own designations, such as the Supply Chain Council's SCOR Professional (SCOR-P) and the Institute of Supply Management's Certified Professional in Supplier Diversity (CPSD).

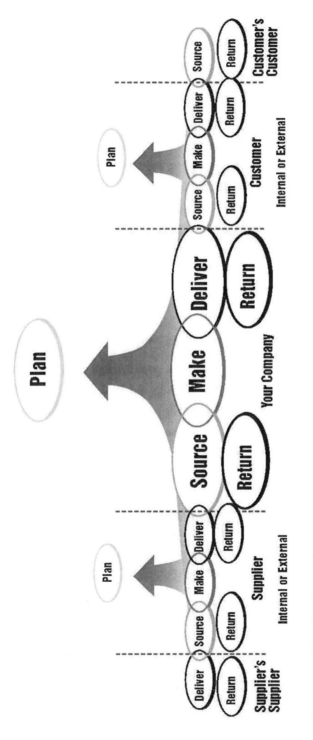

Figure 3.1. The SCOR model.

Source: Supply Chain Council.

Virtual Supply Chains

The concept of virtual supply chains began to arise in the 1990s. As supply chains became more complex, it also became clear that the old models for dealing with suppliers and customers would not work. The lean concept taught practitioners to work more closely with these two groups, and the SCOR model extended this thinking one link further in each direction to the supplier's supplier and the customer's customer. The traditional approach involved legal arrangements for either purchasing from a vendor or supplying a customer. Lean moved away from short-term contracts based solely on price but still involved contracts. Contracts generally involve an agreement over a period of time. In the case of lean, it could be a time period of years rather than months. The German firm Modine, for example, received an 8-year contract to build a factory in Toledo, Ohio, to provide cooling systems for the Jeep plant located there. Without a long-term contract, they would have shipped the cooling units from Germany rather than agreeing to build the plant.[4]

As was discussed in chapter 1, vertical integration is another way of forming long-term relationships with suppliers or customers. Vertical integration, however, involves capital investment, since one must take at least a controlling interest in the firm being vertically integrated. Since capital equipment, particularly at the factory or firm level, is not particularly liquid, the firm must go into vertical integration as a long-term investment. The primary reason firms moved away from vertical integration was to share costs with other links in the supply chain. Without a partner such as Modine, for example, Chrysler would have had to build its own factory to produce cooling systems. In addition to Modine, the Jeep complex actually houses three partners—Kuka, Hyundai, and Magna-Steyr—all operating independently but integrated into the production line.

In many industries, however, the so-called long term is very short. Electronics is a prime example, although there are others. Product life cycles are short, and even if a product appears to be the same to the consumer, the components may change frequently during its life cycle. Consumers now buy more laptop than desktop computers; even smaller netbooks made a big impact in the market as an alternative to standard laptops but were soon challenged by tablet computers starting with the iPad; smartphones are adding capabilities once found only in computers.

The GSM (Global System for Mobile Communications) standard was the original basis for the Apple iPhones, but when Apple moved to include the CDMA (code division multiple access) technology, the internal components were different even though they looked the same to consumers.

To deal with this rapidly changing landscape, virtual supply chains began to arise. A virtual supply chain is a group of firms that are independent but act as if they were a single firm. Penske and the Indian company Genpact are described as "global outsourcing partners [that] work so tightly that they practically are part of the same organization." Genpact is described as a "virtual subsidiary."[5] Although there may be some contractual arrangements among them, often there are not. The reason is flexibility. Firms want to change when the market changes, not when the contracts expire. The firms in a virtual supply chain will share information, including product and production plans, and expect their suppliers to have parts and materials ready when they are needed without the necessity for formal negotiations and agreements. When the market or technology changes, the virtual supply chain has the flexibility to change quickly at the same time. Firms may be added to or leave the virtual supply chain as they are needed or deemed redundant.

Difficulties With Virtual Supply Chains

Although virtual supply chains provide firms flexibility to operate in a changing environment, there are potential difficulties with them. One is trust. The firms in the virtual supply chain must trust each other to consider the welfare of the supply chain as a whole in their decisions and not just the welfare of their individual firms (remember the U.S. Civil War coffee beans example from chapter 1). One of the principles of supply chains is that only the final customer puts new money into the supply chain. All other transactions simply shuffle around existing money.[6] If all firms in the virtual supply chain operated according to this principle, trust would not be a problem. In our accounting systems, however, money is not identified as "new" money or "existing" money; it is just money, and the accounting statements reflect what is happening at the level of the individual firm. In theory, the firms in a virtual supply chain should be sharing costs, profits, and risks. In practice, unless the supply chain firms are vertically integrated into a single firm, this is difficult if not impossible.

The second problem is that virtual supply chains do not exist in isolation. Suppliers often have multiple customers, which means they can be part of multiple virtual supply chains. These supply chains may have differing objectives or may be in competition with one another at some level. Electronics is also a good example here. Although there are many firms offering products in the consumer marketplace, there are relatively few contract manufacturers of everything from materials and components to final products such as laptops. If one traces backward through the supply chains for a Dell or an Acer, for example, at some point or points they will intersect (see chapter 2 for specific examples). Bill Walker, who has written widely about supply-chain management, emphasizes that the supply-chain manager must ask if his or her product line is "simultaneously connected to several supply chain networks that operate differently."[7] So to expect a virtual supply chain to act as if it is a single firm and share costs, profits, and risks raises significant problems if some of the component firms are members of multiple virtual supply chains offering competing products to the final consumers.

A classic example of this phenomenon was Solectron. Solectron was an electronics contract manufacturer supplying most of the firms in the industry, including Cisco, Ericsson, and Lucent. It was a well-run firm and had won two Malcolm Baldrige Awards for quality. In 2001, the industry was clearly experiencing difficulties. Other contract suppliers had spoken out about the problem. "I'm alarmed about the lack of ownership of the massive buildup of inventories," said Harriet Green, an executive at distribution giant Arrow Electronics Inc., which saw its own inventory double in 2000 to $3 billion. "Everyone says it's yours." The suppliers, including Solectron, had been given the production plans for the end users in the virtual supply chains. From the perspective of the suppliers, seeing all the plans, it was clear that the end firms were overly optimistic in terms of both the size of the total market and their own market shares. When they pointed this out to their customers, they were told basically, "trust us." According to Ajay Shah of Solectron, you cannot "sit there and confront a customer and tell him he doesn't know what he's doing with his business." Firms like Solectron and Arrow trusted their customers and increased their orders to their suppliers and inventories to supply the production and marketing plans they had been given. When the dot-com bubble burst in 2001, the customers essentially said, "Sorry, we changed our minds."

Solectron and Arrow ended up with large inventories for which they had no customers. The customers they had trusted no longer wanted them. It was too late for Solectron to cancel its orders to its 4,000 suppliers, and its inventories totaled $4.7 billion.[8] Solectron languished for several years and eventually disappeared, purchased by Flextronics.

A more recent example resulted from the 2010 BP oil spill in the Gulf of Mexico. BP placed and subsequently canceled orders with a dozen or more suppliers who were "suddenly saddled with containers of inventory, canceled orders and no way to pay their mounting bills." This not only affected BP's immediate suppliers but also firms up the entire supply chain.[9]

A third problem is the amount of information available in a virtual supply chain. Although information sharing is essential for a virtual supply chain to function, information has value. Information can range from marketing intelligence, to product plans, to financial information, to intellectual property. As was pointed out in chapter 1, a reason some firms are vertically integrating is to safeguard this information (e.g., Apple safeguarding its intellectual property by moving design in-house). Partners in the virtual supply chains have to trust each other to keep this proprietary information to themselves.

Although it is difficult to find examples in which this has *not* been the case, since firms are reluctant to disclose where they have been wronged, it is easy to find examples of potential problems. TAL Apparel Ltd. of Hong Kong is a contract manufacturer of men's shirts. Through its factories in Southeast Asia, it manufactures one in eight men's shirts sold in the United States. Its customers include JCPenney, J. Crew, Calvin Klein, Banana Republic, Tommy Hilfiger, Liz Claiborne, Ralph Lauren, and Brooks Brothers. Although there has never been a hint of impropriety about TAL, it is easy to see the diligence it must apply in safeguarding marketing and product information for its customers, who are all competitors in the same clothing market.[10]

An example in which the information has been misused is in the growth of the so-called expert networks. It became obvious to mutual funds, research firms, investment bankers, and hedge funds that supply chains contained information that they could use to gain an advantage in their trading of shares. These expert networks grew to gather and disseminate (i.e., sell) information about product plans and finances. This has caused a redefinition of "insider information." It is no longer necessary to find a source inside a firm to get this insider information; the information is available from other members of the supply chain. The U.S. Attorney's office in Manhattan, New York, has redefined insider information to include this information obtained from outside the individual firm but inside the virtual supply chain.[11]

Another example is the so-called spying probe at Renault. The company did not release details, but intellectual property involving its electric cars had been threatened through its subcontractors.[12] This is exactly the reason Apple is bringing more design work in-house. Renault later admitted they had been "tricked."[13] The whole affair has been described as "a case study in corporate paranoia, distracted leadership—and the perceived threat of an advancing China."[14] Clearly, global subcontracting contains risks not present in domestic markets.

A final difficulty is the basic inability to share information and data. As was pointed out earlier in this chapter, firms had problems coordinating information systems in relatively stable supply chains. When the virtual supply chain can change members rapidly, trying to maintain secure communications connections can be more difficult. Trying to get all firms or potential partners in a supply chain to use the same information systems and protocols is virtually impossible.

The Chain Master

Supply chains, virtual or otherwise, do not function automatically. Around 2000, the concept of the "chain master" began to be codified. The chain master is the firm or division that controls the supply chain. Control may range from dictating the flow of goods or services through the chain to being a benign controller by virtue of some characteristic that makes it a controller. Firms are not elected or appointed to the role of chain master. They can emerge as the chain master for any one of a number of reasons:

- *Market share.* A firm may wield power in the chain simply because of its dominance in the market. Suppliers have no choice but to deal with it. A classic example is Walmart, which sells 32% of the disposable diapers in the United

States.[15] Any manufacturer of disposable diapers must deal with Walmart or suffer greatly. One consultant was quoted as saying, "The second worst thing a manufacturer can do is sign a contract with Wal-Mart. The worst? Not sign one."[16]

- *Size*. A firm may not have a dominant market share but may be large enough relative to its suppliers to operate as the chain master. An example is the automobile manufacturers. Chrysler does not dominate its market, but it is still considerably larger than its suppliers. This allows it to dictate many of the terms by which its suppliers will operate. As they outsource more subassemblies and modules to fewer and fewer suppliers, however, they may find their suppliers getting larger and challenging their position as chain master. In 2005, in order to gain bargaining leverage, Lear stopped shipping parts to Chrysler. Chrysler had to get a court order forcing Lear to resume shipment of the parts.[17] Chrysler got its parts, but this was not exactly in the spirit of supply-chain cooperation. Sometimes the same things happen to the larger suppliers. In 2008, Dana Holding Corp., a first-tier supplier for Chrysler and others, had to sue Citation Corp. to force them to ship parts that Dana had ordered. The basic issue was Dana overreaching its chain-master position. A 2004 study by Planning Perspectives Inc. of Birmingham, Michigan, showed that the Japanese manufacturers were less likely than the Americans to abuse their chain-master position. The result was greater cooperation by the suppliers with the Japanese, including collaboration on quality and design.[18]

- *Technology*. A firm may control a vital technology and thus be able to wield the power of a chain master. This control may be through patent protection or through consolidation of suppliers. Many of the chips, circuit boards, and subassemblies in the IT industry are being manufactured by only a few firms. This is because of the specialized knowledge and machinery required to make these parts. When potential chain masters clash, there must be a resolution. Ford, for example, paid Toyota to license its hybrid technology, even though Ford had no intention of using it. The risk of Toyota trying to gain

control of Ford's supply chain by claiming patent infringement
was so great (and potentially too costly and disruptive) that
Ford "paid off" Toyota.

- *Control of channels.* Because of particular marketing and sales
arrangements in a supply chain, one firm may have control of
the channels of distribution. Since the production of products
is meaningless until they are sold, the firm controlling the
channels controls the supply chain. An example is a firm (which
must remain anonymous) that was established in the 1990s as a
subsidiary of a major IT company for the purpose of developing
a new computer accessory. The firm established a well-
organized, efficient supply chain up to the point of distribution.
The company was told by the parent company to use the existing sales force. The salespeople had little interest in selling the
new product, so it failed to capture market share and the supply
chain died. The subsidiary was subsequently disbanded.

In most supply chains, there is a natural chain master, but the firm
does not always step up to perform the chain-master functions. In a
research project in the early 2000s, four firms were studied to determine
their roles in the supply chain. Two were relatively small firms, and two
were large. One of the small firms was in a relatively weak supply chain
in which the natural chain master played a passive role. The result was
difficult production planning and the subsequent buildup of inventories
to compensate for poor planning. The second small firm was the natural
chain master but failed to act in the role. The result in the supply chain
was similar—poor production planning because of a lack of communication among the links in the supply chain and a buildup of inventories in
compensation. The first large firm was described earlier. The chain master
controlled the channels of distribution and did not consider the product
to be sufficiently important, so it failed to get the product to the customers in sufficient numbers to make the supply chain profitable. The second
large firm, in the food industry, was the chain master by virtue of its size. It
was aware of its chain-master role and had people in charge of the supply
chain who understood the role. The result was the sharing of information,
the smooth functioning of the supply and production process, and the
minimization of inventories.[19]

Summary

Supply chains are complex organisms. Managing supply chains involves issues that either might not arise in an internal supply chain or might not arise in the same context or with the same intensity. The effective supply chain manager will do the following:

- Be aware of the evolutionary origins of supply chain management through JIT/lean concepts. The suppliers and customers are partners, not enemies.
- Realize that creating IT links with supply chain partners can be both difficult and risky. They are technically difficult because of partners using different software packages and protocols and risky because now there are more access points to one's data and information.
- Utilize the resources of industry organizations such as the Supply Chain Council. The council, for example, has over 500 performance measures from which one may choose.
- Participate in virtual supply chains with an appreciation of the risks. Virtual supply chains can provide much-needed flexibility but require close monitoring and a lot of trust.
- Exercise authority wisely if you are the chain master. If you are not, encourage the natural chain master to do so.

CHAPTER 4

The Impact of Globalization

Although, as pointed out in chapter 1, global supply chains are not new, they have grown rapidly in the past few decades to the point where they touch all our lives. Thomas Friedman refers to "supply chaining" as one of the 10 forces that flattened the world.[1] The beginnings of the modern era of globalization can be traced to the large-scale entry of the Japanese into the U.S. auto market in the 1970s and the economic opening of China in the 1980s. The *Economist* dates the "tipping point" at which globalization became dominant in world economic affairs to the fall of the Berlin Wall and the opening of Eastern Europe.[2] In essence, the three-world system (developed world, communist world, and developing world) became a two-world system (minus the communist world with a few exceptions, such as Cuba and North Korea). The entrepreneurial energy released by the former-communist, centrally planned economies joining the world economy led to a number of changes: rapid expansion of trading blocs (such as the European Union [EU]), the addition of lower-cost but productive workers to the global work force, and a restructuring of the political landscape. This entrepreneurial energy spilled over into countries such as India and Brazil, which became major players in the global economy (along with Russia and China, the so-called BRIC [Brazil, Russia, India, and China] countries). It is indicative of this restructuring and new energy that these emerging economies were barely touched by the recession of 2008–2009, while the greatest difficulties were encountered in the mature economies of the United States and Western Europe.

Trading Blocs and the EU

One result of this surge in globalization was a renewed emphasis on trade and trading blocs. At the beginning of the Great Depression in the United States, the passage of the Smoot-Hawley Act, supposedly meant to protect U.S. workers, and the subsequent retaliation by our trading partners resulted in average tariffs of around 40%. Needless to say, this had a devastating effect on world trade. These tariffs remained largely in effect until the Kennedy administration in the early 1960s was successful in passing legislation to promote trade. Tariffs began to come down (they are close to an average of 4% today) but were largely negotiated on a bilateral basis one country at a time.

Europe took the lead in forming meaningful trading blocs with the Treaty of Rome and the formation of the Common Market in the late 1950s. This was an expansion of the European Coal and Steel Community formed after World War II. Initially, however, it included only six countries (the so-called inner six), although three of the four largest economies in Western Europe were included (West Germany, France, and Italy) along with the three so-called Benelux countries (Belgium, the Netherlands, and Luxembourg). Charles de Gaulle refused to let Britain join, so the British formed the so-called outer seven with the Scandinavian counties and Switzerland. Trading blocs evolve in steps toward greater integration. The five steps they can follow include the following:[3]

- *Free-trade area.* Members of the free-trade area move to eliminate tariffs and trade barriers with each other but retain the right to set their trade policies with countries outside the area. This leads to greater trade among the members of the area but also to the obvious problem of goods being transshipped through countries with lower trade barriers to those with higher barriers. For example, the members of the British Commonwealth had preferential tariff terms when exporting to Great Britain. This gave then an entrée into the other members of the "outer seven."

- *Customs union.* As (or if) the problem of transshipment grows, the members of the free-trade area will seek to establish a common trade policy toward other countries. This is usually a difficult negotiation since different policies benefit members unequally. Going back to the U.S. Civil War, for example, a secondary issue was tariffs. The North wanted high tariffs to allow their industries to develop, while the South wanted low tariffs since they depended on agricultural exports. This divide between the manufacturing and agricultural sectors continues today in the United States, the EU, and most countries around the world.

- *Common market.* Although a free-trade area allows relatively unfettered trade within the trading bloc, there still tend to be restrictions on the movement of the factors of production—especially labor and capital. A common market should allow the free movement of these factors, but again, it is a difficult negotiation. Workers and trade unions want to protect their jobs from foreign workers, whom they perceive as being willing to work for much less. Countries want to protect their homegrown industries from foreign ownership. Even though the EU has moved far beyond being a common market, it still has not resolved these two issues fully. The United States allows free internal movement of labor and capital but restricts incoming labor and capital, even from its closest trading partners, Canada and Mexico. At one point in the 1980s, when the United States was worried about the economic strength of the Japanese, one or more states in the Midwest forbade the owning of farmland by nonresidents to prevent the Japanese from investing in their land.

- *Economic union.* Economic union implies a full integration of member economies, including common monetary and fiscal policies. The world has yet to see a true, voluntary economic union. There have been involuntary economic unions following military conquests (e.g., Romans, British, Soviets), but typically, independent countries have too many vested interests to yield their economic decision making to a central authority. The EU attempted to form an economic union with the Maastricht Treaty and the introduction of the euro in 1999 but only went half way. The EU established a common monetary policy but only laid out guidelines for fiscal policy. One of the results was the 2010–2011 (and yet to be fully resolved) crisis in the euro zone involving Portugal, Ireland, Greece, and Spain (the so-called PIGS, an acronym obviously not appreciated by the countries involved). In addition, the economic union did not include all the members of the common market (about a third are outside the euro zone), so this created additional political problems.

The introduction of the euro reduced transaction costs, made possible easy price comparisons, eliminated exchange rate risk, and facilitated the trade in goods within the EU; multiple barriers, however, still remained to capital flows, services, and the movement of labor. At the retail level, for example, even after the introduction of the euro, banks still charged "foreign" transaction fees of up to 10% for transferring money from one country to another until the EU stepped in and forced them to stop. Although there is supposed to be free movement of labor across borders, countries are allowed to opt out of this provision and restrict the flow of workers from the new EU members in Eastern Europe. This is sometimes characterized as the "Polish plumber" problem because of the supposed fear of French plumbers that their jobs would be taken by plumbers emigrating from Poland. More recently, the flow of refugees from North Africa has caused some EU countries to restrict all movement across borders.

- *Political union.* Forming a political union implies giving up most or all of a county's sovereignty to a central authority. This happens on rare occasions. The United States, with the adoption of the Constitution in 1789, could be cited as an example. Prior to that, under the Articles of Confederation, it was not clear that a single country would result from the original 13 colonies. Most of the time, the movement is in the opposite direction; countries tend to split apart for economic, political, or ethnic reasons. The list in the last 50 years is long: Pakistan (Bangladesh), Czechoslovakia, Yugoslavia, and Eritrea, to name a few. The list of those that have combined is quite short: perhaps Vietnam and Germany. The EU has a political structure that seems to gain more authority each year, but they are still a long distance from being a political union.

Other European Groups

Although in the United States one tends to look at Europe as a single entity, there are multiple organizations and agreements among different countries in Europe that intersect like the circles in a complex Venn diagram. They all have different but overlapping memberships, different purposes and missions, and thus conflicting objectives. Decisions in one have implications for the others and can cause decision making to be slow and complex. The major eight are the following:

- EU
- Euro zone
- Shengen area (free movement across borders)
- Council of Europe
- European Free Trade Association
- European Economic Area
- EU Customs Union (including potential members of the EU such as Turkey)
- Countries outside the euro zone that may mint euros (e.g., the Vatican and Monaco)

NAFTA

In the United States, the high point of the liberalization of trade was the approval of the North American Free Trade Agreement (NAFTA) among Canada, the United States, and Mexico in the early 1990s. NAFTA can be classified as a free-trade area, although there remain restrictions on the movement of capital, services, and labor. Although NAFTA was and is criticized for eliminating jobs in the United States (referred to in the 1996 U.S. presidential election campaign as "the great sucking sound"), trade among the three virtually exploded after its approval. Trade between the United States and Canada, for example, grew from 37% to 65% of the Canadian GDP in the first 10 years. The United States and Canada have the world's largest trading relationship (although by 2010, China had become the largest source of U.S. imports).[4] In Mexico, NAFTA resulted in the establishment of the maquiladoras manufacturing zone along the U.S. border. Firms invested in factories in this area to take advantage of less-expensive Mexican labor and the relatively free movement across the border. As with all agreements of this type, when protected markets are opened up, some groups suffer and others prosper. There is no doubt that some manufacturing jobs moved from the United States to Mexico. On the other hand, the Mexican market was opened to U.S. goods, especially agriculture. Free trade is not a zero-sum game—both sides benefit, and this was the case with NAFTA. All three partners have grown faster and added more jobs than they would have without the treaty. (It should be pointed out that there is considerable debate on this issue because of the difficulty in isolating the effects of the treaty.) Overall, tariffs have been reduced by about 99% in the first 10 years of the treaty. More than 80% of Mexican and Canadian trade and a third of U.S. trade is among the three partners.

There were several significant restrictions in the treaty. Cross border investment was not allowed in industries such as Mexican oil and railroads, U.S. airlines and communications, and Canadian culture. Although cross border transportation was liberalized, under pressure from the trade unions (and in violation of the treaty), Mexican truck drivers were not allowed to carry goods into the United States (although Canadian truckers were). This issue was finally settled in 2011 after Mexico began imposing significant tariffs on U.S. goods.[5] The biggest obstacle to expanding NAFTA beyond a free-trade area is the movement of labor. Although the problem that gets the most notice in the press is the illegal immigration of Mexicans to the United States, all movement is restricted. After 2001, for security reasons, simply crossing the borders became more difficult, with travelers required to present passports to cross. So the United States has moved from virtually restriction-free travel between the United States and Canada to requiring either a passport or a federal ID card to cross borders. This is in contrast to the EU in this time period, which has largely eliminated cross border checks within the Shengen area.

Because of political resistance to NAFTA in the United States, the expansion of free trade slowed, especially in the first decade of the 21st century. Most expansions have been bilateral negotiations, such as those with Colombia and South Korea. The economic downturn of 2008–2009 generated further resistance to free trade and increased pressure for economic isolation in the belief that this would protect jobs.

Other Trading Blocs

There are a multiplicity of trading blocs around the world. Africa is a constantly changing mosaic of trade areas. Central and South America have Mercosur, the Andean Pact, and the Central American Common

Market. In Asia, the most prominent is the Association of Southeast Asian Nations (ASEAN), which includes 10 Southeast Asian countries but does not include the Chinese economic powerhouses of the People's Republic of China, Hong Kong, and Taiwan.

WTO

Overlaying the formation of trading blocs was the creation of the World Trade Organization (WTO) in 1995 to replace the post–World War II General Agreement on Trade and Tariffs (GATT). The members of the WTO, which include most of the trading nations in the world, agreed to continue to reduce tariffs and trade restrictions. The most significant provision in the WTO was the formation of enforcement procedures against antitrade actions. Although it is somewhat ironic, countries violating the free-trade agreements can be punished by having restrictions imposed on them. In other words, free-trade restrictions can be punished by further free-trade restrictions. A prominent case has been the United States and the EU each bringing a case to the WTO claiming that the other has "unfairly" subsidized the development of large commercial aircraft (Boeing in the United States and Airbus in the EU). Both were found to be at fault, although at the time of this writing, the cases have not been fully resolved. While the WTO has brought more order to world trade and has put downward pressure on tariffs and other restrictions, there are still serious unresolved issues. The most important is agriculture. The developing countries want free trade in agriculture since that is their main economic strength, while the developed countries have strong agricultural political lobbies wanting to restrict trade and continue agricultural subsidies. In the EU, for example, agricultural subsidies represent around 48% of the budget (down from around 90% in the 1970s) even though agriculture is 2% of its GDP and 3.7% of its employment.[6] Other issues involve intellectual property rights and free trade in services.

In the context of global supply chains, trading blocs are a two-edged sword. On the positive side, the free movement of goods means that a firm may choose where to produce within the bloc without regard to the borders and serve the entire market within the bloc from one location. This is especially true in the euro zone, where the common currency has eliminated transactions costs and exchange-rate risks. The downside to trading blocs is that they may form a customs union and restrict trade by their members with other countries or blocs. With the WTO supposedly guarding against the traditional forms of restrictions, countries and blocs become more creative. An example is the restrictions in the EU against the sale of genetically modified food products, even though they are widely used in the rest of the world.[7]

In the midst of this growth of trading blocs and the creation of the WTO, China has emerged as a major economic force. China is now the second-largest economy in the world, having passed Japan.[8] China is the largest source of imports for the United States and the third-largest destination for exports (after Canada and Mexico). Likewise, the United States is China's largest export destination (but only its fourth-largest source of imports).[9] Considering that trade with China was virtually zero in 1980, this growth has been explosive.

Impact on Principles of Operations Management

All these developments have had an impact on the management of global supply chains. The various bodies of knowledge in operations management and just-in-time (JIT)/lean contained a number of principles that have been seriously challenged by the growth of global supply chains. The basis of these principles is the list of seven wastes that are part of the lean system:[10]

1. Overproduction
2. Waiting time
3. Unnecessary transportation
4. Excess processing
5. Too much inventory
6. Unnecessary motion
7. Defects

The Seven Wastes

Although the seven wastes were developed with internal production in mind, they are as applicable and just as wasteful in a global context.

1. *Overproduction.* A firm may order more than is actually needed to meet a transportation requirement such as filling a container. Or it may order more safety stock to guard against quality problems or receiving the wrong goods.

2. *Waiting time.* Failure to receive an order because of transportation delays or natural disasters (such as earthquakes) may cause machine downtime.

3. *Unnecessary transportation.* We shall cover this important waste in the next section and in chapter 7.

4. *Excess processing.* Shipping though ports adds days to processing in both the sending and receiving countries (see chapter 5).

5. *Too much inventory.* If you have inventory in the pipeline from China, you own that inventory. We shall have more to say on this later.

6. *Unnecessary motion.* There is an example in chapter 7 of a quality manager who had to fly to China to investigate a problem with a supplier. It involved a lot of unnecessary motion (and expense).

7. *Defects.* Defects are no more likely to occur in a global supply chain, but correcting problems may take significantly more time and expense.

Unnecessary Transportation

The most significant challenge of global supply chains has been "unnecessary transportation." Firms using lean management principles sought to reduce transportation pipelines both inside the firm and with suppliers. In the example of Modine and Chrysler mentioned earlier, by offering Modine a long-term contract, Chrysler was able to shorten its pipeline from a container trip from Germany to a short drive in the same industrial park.

As the lure of lower labor costs in Asia, and especially China, beckoned to many firms, this principle was often ignored. The average transit time for a container from China to the United States, for example, is 45 days, assuming no problems en route.[11] Someone has to own the pipeline inventory during that transit time. Using the generally accepted U.S. average inventory holding cost of 35%, that transit time alone adds at least 5% to the cost of the items.

Ohio Art Case

An example of a firm that moved its production to China based on lower labor costs but failed to anticipate other difficulties is Ohio Art, the maker of the children's toy Etch A Sketch.[12] Because of price pressures from its customers, most notably the retailers Walmart and Target, Ohio Art was forced to sell its product at less than half of the 1960 price on an inflation-adjusted basis. The lure of 24-cents-per-hour labor (vs. $9 per hour in Ohio) was too much, so the company signed a contract to move its production to China in the early 2000s. This lengthened its supply chain significantly (principle 3). The long supply chain meant that Ohio Art had to extend its sales forecast horizon. A longer forecast horizon means greater uncertainty. Erring on the high side to avoid running out means a greater likelihood of excess production and too much inventory (principles 1 and 5). Shipping by sea involves extra processing (principle 4) and motion (principle 6). During the lead-up to the 2004 Christmas season, its shipments were held up because of a trade-union strike at the Port of Long Beach (principle 2). Because the company contracted for production and had no one on site in China, it also lost control of the production process and could not determine the quality of the production until the containers arrived in Bryan, Ohio (principle 7). In addition to its problems with lean principles, Ohio Art trusted its Chinese contractor implicitly, much to its chagrin. The *New York Times* visited China and did an exposé on Ohio Art for underpaying (even by Chinese standards) and mistreating the workers. It is difficult to put a price on the bad publicity it received as a result of this exposé.

The Bullwhip Effect in Global Supply Chains

One of the most widely used exercises in operations and supply-chain management classes in U.S. universities is a simulation known as the beer game. It was developed in the 1950s at MIT and is intended to illustrate the impact of communication on the effective management of a supply chain (although the term was not even in use in the 1950s). The principle underlying the simulation is that small changes in retail demand ripple through a wholesaler, distributor, and manufacturer, causing ever wilder gyrations in orders and production as one moves upstream in the supply chain (see Figure 4.1).

If the participants are not allowed to communicate with each other except through written orders, these wild gyrations are, in fact, what happens every time the simulation is run. This is known as the "bullwhip" effect. With an actual bullwhip, small movements in the handle (customer orders) result in rapid and sudden movements in the tip of the whip (the manufacturers), causing the characteristic "snap." If the participants in the simulation are allowed to communicate with each other, the process becomes smooth and functions well. The point is that constant communication among all members of the supply chain is necessary for it to operate smoothly. The bullwhip effect is not just a game, however. At the beginning of 2010, the *Wall Street Journal* reported on the bullwhip effect on firms, such as Caterpillar, beginning to rebuild their inventories.[13] The real bullwhip effect followed the same pattern as the simulation. In the final quarter of 2008, consumer purchases of electronics gear fell 9%, factory shipments fell 10%, and the production of chips that went into the

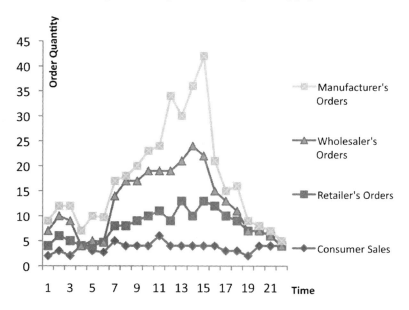

Figure 4.1. The bullwhip effect.

devices fell 20%—a classic case of the bullwhip effect.[14] Controlling the bullwhip effect in global supply chains is a significantly greater problem than controlling it domestically.

One way to enhance communication and thus control the fluctuations in the supply chain is to have the participants close to each other. Too much transportation (principle 3), as in global trade, means they are not close enough. Longer supply chains with participants in different countries mean poorer communication (for a number of reasons discussed in the next chapter), which means a supply chain is subject to erratic and large fluctuations. Measuring the costs involved in these fluctuations is difficult (e.g., excess inventory and poor customer service), which is why many firms ignore or pay little attention to them. The costs are there, however, and they do affect the bottom line.

Summary

The rapid development of globalization has had impacts throughout the global economy down to the management of individual businesses. The global landscape continues to change rapidly. As a supply-chain manager, you should remain constantly aware of the following:

- Developments in trading blocs, the WTO, bilateral negotiations, and trade policy in general taking advantage of opportunities when they arise.
- What is happening in China, without becoming mesmerized. China has its own problems, such as a rapidly aging population, which can cause sudden changes in its economic situation.
- The rise of other countries such as Indonesia, India, and emerging African countries.
- How lengthening supply chains will affect your costs and the ability to manage your business effectively.
- What the impact of globalization will be on your efforts to create a "lean" organization.

CHAPTER 5

Globalization Issues

Firms entering the global economy generally face a wide range of issues not faced when they operate domestically—issues such as time, language, culture, and ethics in addition to infrastructure, government policies, and money.

Time

Firms extending their supply chains to Asia face time differences of up to 12 hours and even different days (because of the international date line). This means that if direct communication is to take place, someone must be working outside his or her normal working hours. Some Indian IT companies have located their call centers in countries in South America, such as Paraguay and Uruguay, to be closer to the eastern U.S. time zone. A German consulting firm with which the author was familiar actively sought business in South Africa to eliminate the time zone effect (i.e., jet lag) in its global activities. Electronic communication makes communication across time zones easier, but there still may be delays of a day or more. Simply picking up the phone and calling someone is not always feasible. If a supplier is located across the street, you always have the option of walking over there and discussing a problem on the spot. If the supplier is in China, it may take several days to even establish the nature of the problem.

Language

Language is a problem Americans often ignore on the assumption that everyone speaks English. English has become the universal language of business, but that does not mean that everyone speaks English or speaks it fluently. Even among those who speak it fluently, there can be significant differences. For example, "pipped at the post," meaning defeated or nosed out at the last minute, is a common expression in Australia, but it is unknown in the United States. Accents may differ and lead to misunderstandings. Americans are often exhorted to learn more languages, but the question remains which to learn. Should one learn Chinese because of the size of their economy (although there was no rush to learn Japanese when Japan was the second-largest economy)? Should one learn a European language (even though English has become a common language in the EU)? A survey of U.S. firms projected that between 2010 and 2020, the languages other than English that will be most in demand are Spanish, Chinese, Arabic, and Russian.[1] Translation is always available, even online, but it is not always reliable. Getting documents correct can be critical. The most effective way to ensure that documents are correct is to have them double translated—for example, from English to Chinese and then back again. Comparing the two English versions will highlight any problems. In any event, a native speaker should edit all translated documents. First Solar Inc., for example, has mandated English as the official language of the company. This means that all management communications are carried out in English. All shop-floor instruction manuals are translated into the local languages, however.

Culture

Culture and ethics are often two big sticking points in dealing with global supply-chain partners. The two issues are often considered together, although, for the most part, they are two different issues. There is nothing ethical about how to present a business card, and there is nothing cultural about murder. Culture is a complex subject that could fill an entire book in itself. The focus here will be on some of the issues that may arise in managing global supply chains.

Culture is determined by five factors[2]:

- Religion
- Political and economic philosophies
- Education
- Language
- Social structure

Religion

The cultural factors are not equal in all situations and often have an impact where one does not expect them. Religion is probably the most pervasive factor in that it tends to transcend the others. Changes in governments, economic systems, or education systems tend to have little effect on underlying religious values. Governments, for example, may encourage or suppress religion but seldom have a long-term effect on its practice. The question for the manager of a global supply chain is how important religion is in a particular country or region. In Germany, for example, religion is a minor (or nonexistent) factor in business dealings. In the Middle East, it may be of overriding importance. Religion may appear in unexpected situations. In greeting rituals, for example, a Hindu woman may decline to shake hands with a man (or a Hindu man may decline to shake hands with a woman). This practice is rooted in religion but expresses itself in the common practice of whether or not to shake hands. Religion may contribute to the degree of collectivism or individualism in society and thus affect the nature of business negotiations.

The Political and Economic Philosophies

The political and economic philosophies in a society can affect the culture, although they may not be as deep rooted as religion. In extreme cases, the political and economic philosophies in North Korea and Cuba certainly affect the culture of doing business. These are apparently imposed from above but could change rapidly, as evidenced by South Korea having a radically different business culture from North Korea. When the countries of Eastern Europe were in the Soviet bloc, they had a collectivist economic and political culture. When the so-called iron curtain fell, most of these countries changed rapidly to a more individualistic and private-market culture.

Education

Although the role of education is normally thought of as teaching the basics of math, science, language, art, and social science, the educational system has a major role in teaching culture. Children are taught to be in school at the same time every day and to stay there until they are dismissed, just as they will be required to do when they enter the workforce. They are taught (we hope) to be respectful to their elders and about the common history and lore of their country or region. They are taught the common language of their country. Education may not create culture, but it is a powerful force for the transmission and perpetuation of it.

Language

Language can reflect cultural values and particularly social structure. In the United States, people tend to be quite informal in business dealings, often using first names (perhaps to excess) with people they do not know well. Such a practice would be a grave social error in countries such as Japan or even Germany. In Germany, for example, their language has different forms of the pronoun "you" depending on how well one knows the person. Using the familiar instead of the formal form of "you" with a relative stranger can be considered an insult (as would using the formal with a close acquaintance).

Social Structure

Countries with a history of social strata may retain vestiges of these strata even if they have been outlawed. In India, for example, castes still exist even though it may be illegal to consider them in business dealings. In other cultures, women may have a different social status than men. Race and ethnicity may be involved in local hiring decisions. It is often a difficult decision for a manager to know how or even if to consider such factors in business decisions. What appears to be a cultural decision may, in fact, turn out to be an ethical decision.

Cultural Training

For the manager going abroad, or even dealing with business partners from other countries, cultural training is a must. Some global firms, such as the Swiss bank UBS AG, provide a detailed cultural guide for their employees, offering advice such as to "never reject an invitation to the sauna" when in Russia.[3] Any local university with a business school will have experts in international business who can provide cultural training. Fortunately, self-study in this area has been made easy. Marshall Cavendish Books publishes a "Culture Shock" series of books on a number of countries. They do not prepare one for everything, but they do give a good background. Another aid is the *International Herald Tribune*. Each Monday it prints a list of the countries that have holidays that week (meaning businesses may be closed). Every day is a holiday somewhere in the world! (The information is also available from sources such as Bloomberg and Reuters.) From time to time, publications such as the *Wall Street Journal* will offer cultural tips.[4] Robert J. Trent and Llewellyn R. Roberts's book *Managing Global Supply Chain and Risk* has a chapter on subjects such as greeting rituals and gift giving.[5] If you are responsible for a particular country or area, buy a local calendar that has its holidays. This can save you from a lot of missed appointments, poor scheduling, and social gaffes.

A helpful step can be to join a service club such as Rotary, Kiwanis, Lions, or Zonta. These are organizations of professional people and have chapters in virtually every country in the world. When you visit or move to another country, you will have an instant network of professionals and access to people who can be mentors or answer your cultural questions. No matter where you are, when you go to a meeting (which you can do without an invitation), you are immediately welcome. No one will question why you are there.

Always be aware that countries do not always have common cultures within their borders. In the United States, New York City; Austin, Texas; and San Francisco have vast cultural differences. The Bavarians in Germany are distinct from the Berliners. The Scots and the English are different. Fortunately, everyone operating in a global environment faces the same dilemmas and questions no matter what his or her country of origin. The person who is flexible and willing to learn succeeds the best. The president of PharmaSecure, commenting on their success abroad, noted that "the company's ease and comfort working across cultures [has been important]."[6]

Decision Sharpness Example

An example that illustrates the issues with time, language, and culture, as well as some of the lean issues discussed in the previous chapter, can be referred to as the "decision sharpness" example. The definition and metric of decision sharpness is the interval between the point in time when a decision maker realizes he or she needs to make a decision and the point in time when there is enough information to make it. The example (a true story) involves deciding if there is enough inventory on hand to continue production or if the item needs to be reordered.

The supply-chain manager in New Jersey wanted to increase the production schedule at a plant in Malaysia. The supplier of the parts he needed was in the Netherlands. The supplier in the Netherlands was a subsidiary of a company in Germany, so he had to go through the chain of command (an effect of long supply chains). At 9:00 a.m. on a Friday, he called the Germans to ask them to call the Dutch to determine the number of items in inventory. It was, however, 15:00 (3:00 p.m.) in Germany (time differences), and German firms typically do not answer the phones after 14:00 (2:00 p.m.) on Fridays because the secretaries have left for the day. So he got no answer. He called again on Monday, but it was a holiday in Germany, so no one was at work (differences in culture). He called again on Tuesday, and the Germans readily agreed to forward his request to the Dutch. The Dutch are not predisposed to taking orders from Germans, so they put off checking the inventory level until Wednesday (culture). They discovered that they did not use the same nomenclature and stock-keeping units (SKUs) as the Americans, so they had to check the inventory manually instead of on the computer (language, measurement, and computer system differences). They sent the answer to the Germans, who forwarded it to the United States. On Friday, a decision-sharpness gap of 7 days, the supply-chain manager in New Jersey had his answer. The result was that the factory in Malaysia ran out of parts and had to stop production. If the inventory had been in New Jersey, or if the supply chain had been internal and they had used an ERP system, the decision-sharpness factor would have been 5 minutes. Instead, a global supply chain using external suppliers stretched the decision-sharpness factor to 7 days.

The supply-chain manager who related the story said that the situation was even more complicated than it sounds. The headquarters for the company owning the Malaysian factory was in Hong Kong; the headquarters company was a subsidiary of a firm in Singapore that had a U.S. sales office in California. So his communication chain with the factory in Malaysia went through California, Singapore, and Hong Kong and finally to Malaysia. This involved at least three languages and multiple time zones. The cost savings from cheaper labor by producing in Malaysia was clear and easy to calculate; the cost of complicated communication lines and the lack of decision sharpness is something that does not typically appear in the accounting statements.

Ethics

Ethics is also a multifaceted subject that could occupy whole chapters and books. It covers everything from basic taboos such as killing and stealing to grayer areas such as bribery. To complicate things further, a matter such as bribery can range from excessive tipping to large kickbacks on contracts. A good global business textbook—such as Charles W. L. Hill's *Global Business Today*[7] or John Wild, Kenneth Wild, and Jerry Han's *International Business*[8]—can lay out the issues. Ethics has been in the foundations of capitalism from the beginning. Adam Smith was a moral philosopher, and before he wrote *The Wealth of Nations*, he wrote *The Theory of Moral Sentiments*. Ethics and moral behavior were a prerequisite to his system of laissez-faire economics.

The first guideline for the global supply-chain manager is to be legal. Be legal in your home country and be legal in your host country. The United States has a Foreign Corrupt Practices Act, making bribery illegal anywhere in the world. (The U.S. Department of Justice initiated 150 cases under this act in 2010.) The Organization for Economic Cooperation and Development (OECD) has a Convention on Combating Bribery of Foreign Officials in International Business Transactions[9] that has been signed by 38 countries. The German-based company Siemens, for example, has paid more than $1.6 billion in fines to the United States and German governments for corrupt practices. The U.S. company Johnson & Johnson paid $70 million to the United States and the United Kingdom because of the payment of bribes and kickbacks.[10] New cases appear almost weekly in the business media.

The second guideline is to have an organizational code of ethics: "Companies need to develop explicit codes of conduct on corruption, train their staff to handle demands for pay-offs and back them up when they refuse them."[11] Be sure that your company culture is one that demands ethical behavior and that everyone, from the CEO to the lowest-paid worker, behaves ethically and expects ethical behavior from others.

Finally, one should have a personal code of ethical conduct. There are some who would argue that ethical behavior depends on where you are—that different countries and cultures have different ethical standards. A counter to this argument is that the service organizations mentioned earlier have codes of ethical behavior that every member in the world agrees to follow. There are no cultural exceptions, no equivocation. Rotary, for example, has a "Four Way Test"[12] that all members, in every culture and country, agree to follow:

1. Is it the TRUTH?
2. Is it FAIR to all concerned?
3. Will it build GOODWILL and BETTER FRIENDSHIPS?
4. Will it be BENEFICIAL to all concerned?

Since Rotary has members in virtually every country in the world, you can find professionals around the world who profess to adhere to the same code of ethics.

Development and Infrastructure

The state of development and the infrastructure are important factors to consider in deciding whether to move into the global economy and where. A country attractive for its low wages may not have the port facilities, for example, to move raw materials in and finished goods out of the country. Transportation to and from the port may be difficult because of the lack of good roads, railroads, or canals. Or a poor transportation system may make it difficult for workers to get to work. It is not unheard of for a company to establish an internal bus system to get its employees to and from work. A poorly organized banking system may make it difficult to transfer funds or even to pay workers and suppliers.

The state of development is an issue in several ways. In developed countries, one assumes that if there is a need for raw materials, parts, or subassemblies, then there will be a vendor available to supply these items who will charge a reasonable price and deliver within a reasonable time. In a developing country, none of these may be true. The classic story is when McDonald's entered Russia for the first time: They had to buy and develop the entire supply chain to ensure the quantity and quality of their beef, potatoes, and other components.

One might think that communications would be difficult in developing countries, but a phenomenon sometimes known as "generation skipping" makes many of them more advanced than the United States in telephone communications. Landlines have long been a bottleneck in communications in developing countries. Most telephone companies have been state monopolies. This meant a poor response to customer needs and politicization of the management process. Even where sufficient lines were erected, the cost was high and the wires were frequently stolen for their copper. Starting in the 1990s, however, the introduction of mobile telephony in the developing countries has revolutionized communications there. They are able to skip over landlines and the early technology in mobile phones. Mobile phones have spread so rapidly that many economists have estimated that they add 0.8% or more to the growth rate in developing countries.[13] Communication allows better access to information such as crop prices and better efficiency by enhancing communications with suppliers and customers. People in villages act as "walking phone booths" by selling use of a phone by the minute to their neighbors. Mobile minutes are used as a faux currency since they can be transported easily electronically. Mobile phone companies have responded by redesigning transmission towers (e.g., to use solar energy) and phones (to reduce their cost) and changing the cost structure of adding time to a call plan. In Germany, for example, the least-expensive

Table 5.1. Advantages and Disadvantages of Global Supply Chains

Advantages	Disadvantages
Lower costs	Long supply chains
Centralized functions	Exchange rate risk
Economies of scale	Remoteness from customers
Local talents	Transportation arrangements
	Cultural differences
	Political unrest
	Decisions not "sharp"

plan for adding minutes to a prepaid SIM card costs about €15 (about $20). In India, one can add minutes for 100 rupees (about $2). In Kenya, competition has driven the cost of a text message down to one cent.[14] The mobile infrastructure has been relatively immune to damage since, it seems, even criminals and terrorists use mobile phones. In short, what once was a significant disadvantage of operating in a developing country has become a distinct advantage.

The Impact of Governmental Policies

Governments can be a significant issue in globalization. Aside from the issues of stability, corruption, and political philosophy, there are a number of areas that can have a major impact on a firm looking to locate in a particular country. The first is the ease of starting a business. The irony is that the countries that need new businesses the most are those in which it is most difficult to get one started. According to the World Bank,[15] 7 of the 10 countries in which it was most difficult to start a new business were in Africa (an improvement from 9 out of 10 the year before). The easiest was New Zealand (the United States was ninth). One day was required in New Zealand to start a business; Haiti required 105, and Suriname required 694 (the United States required 6). Starting a business involves everything from obtaining capital to obtaining construction permits. It is little wonder that the developed countries are more likely to attract foreign direct investment than the developing countries. The World Bank report is a good reference rating countries on nine different dimensions of the ease of doing business.

All governments control trade: from tariffs, to quotas, to embargoes, to administrative requirements. Sometimes governments seek to promote trade with subsidies or free-trade zones, but most often they seek to restrict it by imposing costs, direct controls, or bureaucratic requirements. Although average tariffs and restrictions have been reduced dramatically since the 1950s, individual countries differ widely in their treatment of trade. The World Bank[16] ranked countries based on the time, cost, and number of documents required to import or export a full 20-foot container (the 20-foot equivalent unit [TEU] standard). The two easiest countries were Singapore and Hong Kong. The bottom 10 were all developing countries in Africa and Asia. Table 5.2 is a sample of countries

Table 5.2. Ease of Exporting

Country	Rank	Days to export	Documents needed	Cost ($)
Singapore	1	5	4	456
Hong Kong	2	6	4	625
Germany	14	7	4	872
USA	20	6	4	1050
China	50	21	7	500
Niger	174	59	9	3545
Burkina Faso	175	41	10	2412
Congo, Republic	180	50	11	3818
Kazakhstan	181	81	10	3005
Cent. African Rep.	182	54	9	5491

Source: World Bank.

to show the wide differences.[17] Since greater exports are a national policy in most countries, only the data for exporting are shown.

It is clear from Table 5.2 that a lack of economic development is more a cause of low levels of exports than a result. It is also clear that trade brokers to help negotiate one's way through the export process are necessary for a company that wishes to participate in the global economy. Trading in the world economy is far more complex than trading domestically. One should enter the arena with caution and be fully prepared. Fortunately, brokers are available, and governments, from the local to the federal level, are eager to help businesses that wish to export. One such broker specializing in small businesses—High Street Partners Inc. of Annapolis, Maryland—has been working with more than 300 small firms. The president commented, "There's an explosion of 50- to 100-person companies that are going overseas. We're not even scratching the surface."[18]

One way to avoid the problems of importing and exporting is to produce in the countries where one's markets are located. Some countries may require this as a condition of trade (Airbus produces the A320 airplane in China, for example, as a condition of selling them to the Chinese), but it is one way of moving behind tariff and quota barriers as well as avoiding the time, cost, and bureaucracy of importing and exporting. The other factors mentioned (infrastructure, communications, etc.) may come into play, so it is a matter of balancing the plusses and minuses.

Money

The final globalization issue discussed here is money. The history of money is complex, and its roles are many. An elementary economics textbook is a good place to review the fundamentals. Money is another area that involves governments. Although the U.S. dollar is the primary reserve currency in the world, other currencies, such as the euro, the British pound, the Swiss franc, and the Chinese yuan, either are growing in importance or, in the case of the pound sterling, have been important reserve currencies in the past. Any company trading in the global economy takes on the additional headache of managing currency risk. In the post-GATT (General Agreement on Trade and Tariffs) world, in which gold is no longer a currency standard and the major currencies float freely in value on world markets, dealing with currency risk has become a major part of engaging in world trade. A strong domestic currency encourages imports and direct investment in other countries. A weak currency encourages exports and direct investment in the home country.

Currency Risk

Currency risk appears at three levels: transaction, translation, and economic risks. A firm encounters *transaction risk* each time it exchanges one currency for another. This may be a direct exchange, or it may be buying or selling goods in another currency. On the individual level, for example, a U.S. tourist who travels to a euro zone country with a credit card and a bank debit card will encounter transaction risk each time he or she withdraws cash from a money machine or pays for something with the credit card. The exchange rate could change dramatically from transaction to transaction. This does not happen often, but in the summer of 1973, for example, the U.S. dollar did fall dramatically in value, and many U.S. tourists in Europe were left without enough money to buy a train ticket back to the airport to fly home. The tourist who buys euros before leaving the United States incurs transaction risk only one time because he or she has locked in the exchange rate. A business faces the same risks, but a change in currency value is more likely to happen because the time between agreeing to buy or sell goods and the time payment takes place can span weeks or months.

A firm that incurs no transaction risk may still face *translation risk*. It is possible for a U.S. firm to have branches in multiple countries where all suppliers and customers are domestic. At the end of the year, however, the firm must convert its financial statements into dollars for a number of reasons, not the least of which is paying taxes. A changing exchange rate can have a dramatic effect on the firm's bottom line, even though no currencies have actually been converted into dollars. The firm faces the same risk when repatriating profits.

Finally, a firm operating in the global economy faces *economic risk* in the long term. Although a strong domestic currency may encourage investment abroad, investment typically takes time to complete and is intended to stay in place for several years. Factories cannot be moved around like people. The economic risk is that an investment abroad that seems to be a good idea one year may, in fact, turn out to be a bad idea by the time the investment is complete because of exchange rate fluctuations. Investing abroad is a matter of good forecasting and risk management.

The global landscape is quite complicated in terms of currency even when one considers only market fluctuations in exchange rates. This is an area, however, where government intervention is pervasive and constant. Although the major currencies in the world have their exchange rates determined by the market, the majority of countries (over 80%) use some kind of government intervention to control the rate. They may have pegged rates or currency boards to attempt to keep the rate constant with respect to a major currency. From a business point of view, this is desirable since it guarantees the exchange rate (with the major peg) as long as the peg does not change. For example, until 2010, China generally kept the yuan pegged to the dollar. The yuan still fluctuated with regard to other currencies such as the euro and Japanese yen. Governments may use exchange rates to try to enforce political or economic policies. In 2010, Venezuela, for example, had four different exchange rates ranging from the official rate of 4.3 bolivars per dollar to the 8.0 black-market rate. They also had a rate of 2.3 for importing food and medicines and

5.3 for buying dollars for business. Some countries may allow conversion only one way—from a major currency into theirs but not back again.

It is difficult to overstate the importance of managing currency risk when operating in the global economy. For Toyota, for example, a one-yen appreciation against the dollar reduces annual operating profits by $450 million![19] In 2004, Volkswagen's first-quarter profits dropped by €300 million because of unfavorable exchange rates.[20] In Canada, for every one cent the loonie (Canadian dollar) strengthens, their manufacturers lose about C$1.5 billion per year. When the U.S. dollar collapsed in 2007, Standen's Ltd. of Canada saw the value of their U.S. sales drop below profitability in the 60 days they allowed their customers to pay their bills.[21] The CEO of Christie Digital Systems Canada Inc. reports using aggressive hedging and strategies to minimize exchange-rate risk (such as sourcing in U.S. dollars and selling in Canadian dollars). Despite their efforts, every one-cent change in the exchange rate has a 1% impact on their bottom line.[22] Clearly, exchange-rate risk demands one's attention and efforts to mitigate it.

Purchasing Power Parity (PPP)

The question faced by every currency-risk manager is what the exchange rate should be. Knowing this can tell one if a currency is over- or under-valued and help with forecasting exchange rates. There are two primary factors determining the exchange rate between two currencies at any given time. One is the relative purchasing power of the currencies in their home economies. This is what the exchange rate should be. The other is speculation. Virtually all the day-to-day changes in exchange rates are caused by speculation. (See Figure 5.1.) For the manager trying to forecast the medium- to long-term movements in the value of a currency, the difference between these two rates is key information. The speculative value is the market-exchange rate (or, in the case of nonfloating currencies, whatever the government in question says it is). This information is easy to find. The most common measure of the underlying exchange rate based on purchasing power is called purchasing power parity (PPP). Except in cases of rapid inflation or deflation, PPP is relatively stable. (Again, see Figure 5.1.) The difficulty is measuring it. Economists have devoted a lot of energy trying to construct good measures of PPP. To construct PPP,

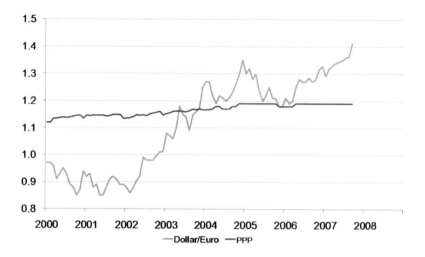

Figure 5.1. The effect of speculation on exchange rates.

Source: Volksbank Bad Mergentheim, eG.

one must compare identical goods in different countries. Finding goods that are identical around the world is difficult. In the 1990s, the *Economist*, in a self-described "light-hearted" attempt, constructed a PPP index using the Big Mac hamburger from McDonald's. Except where eating beef is taboo (such as among Hindus in India), beef is eaten around the world, and the Big Mac is virtually identical in its presentation and distribution.[23] From an economist's point of view, the fatal flaw is that the Big Mac Index contains only one item. On the other hand, experience has proven the Big Mac Index to be remarkably accurate in determining if the market value of a currency is over- or undervalued compared to its PPP value. In addition to its accuracy, it is readily available and easy to understand. By looking at the Big Mac Index, a manager can make a reasonably accurate judgment about future movements of a currency's value relative to the U.S. dollar (or, by inference, any other currency). There are two major caveats: No index is 100% accurate, so while the direction of the movement may be fairly certain, the size of the movement may be less so. The other caveat is that knowing *if* a currency will change in value does not indicate *when* it will change. This is a matter of the manager's forecasting judgment (and perhaps luck).

There are many ways to mitigate exchange-rate risk; detailed explanations can be found in the finance literature. The following are some of the most common and easiest to implement:

- Purchase forward contracts to lock in your exchange rate. This can be done through a bank or broker.
- If you do a lot of business in a particular country or area, keep a bank account in that currency to eliminate some of the transaction risk caused by multiple currency exchanges.
- Maintain a facility in a country where you are selling. This allows you to make more of your transactions in that currency and avoid transaction risk.

Doing nothing is the same thing as speculation. You put yourself at the mercy of the currency market and the speculators. Taking basic steps to mitigate currency risk is relatively easy, even for a small business.

Summary

Be aware of the issues you will face when you are part of a global supply chain. Every country or region is different. According to the MIT global risk survey,

> Every region of the world has its own supply chain risk profile and unique sensitivity to the threat of disruption. For example, Africans do not perceive hurricanes or earthquakes as major supply chain hazards, but are wary of product tampering and currency devaluations. Managers in India are more concerned about infestations and civil unrest than hurricanes. In China, earthquakes and counterfeit products are seen as likely threats to the integrity of supply chains.[24]

The perception of earthquakes may change in the United States after the 2011 earthquakes in Japan shut down some important supply chains.[25] In fact, in an article in *Barron's*, Alan Abelson, quoting Stephanie Pomboy, speculates that with the earthquakes in Japan and the political turmoil in the Middle East and northern Africa, the age of globalization may be coming to an end. Companies may decide that the risks and costs of global supply chains are too great and may shorten their supply chains[26] (in a manner similar to the examples in chapter 7).

Allow time to prepare yourself for managing in the global arena:

- Join a service club to give you instant access to a professional network no matter where in the world you happen to be.
- Take training in the culture and language of the countries and companies where you do business; give the same training to your employees.
- Know the law when it comes to ethics. Know and follow your company's and your own ethical codes no matter where you are.
- Keep a clock (or clocks) on your wall showing the time in the regions where you do business (the kind of display you see in airports and hotels that cater to international customers).
- Get a calendar from the region(s) where you do business so you are aware of holidays.
- Take advantage of sources such as the World Bank and the *Economist* to learn "the numbers" of the countries where you do business.
- Learn the risks particular to the country or region where you are doing business.
- Develop reliable communication channels.
- Manage your currency risk; don't speculate (doing nothing amounts to speculation).

CHAPTER 6

Supply-Chain Security

A 2007 column in the *Wall Street Journal* urged executives to focus on four priorities based on the events of the summer of 2007. At the top of the list was "make supply-chain management a top priority." The story went on to say, "Don't wait for a crisis."[1] Much of the story focused on supply-chain security. In 2011, Janet Napolitano, the U.S. secretary of homeland security, wrote an op-ed piece in the *Wall Street Journal* titled "How to Secure the Global Supply Chain."[2]

There has been a lot written on supply-chain vulnerability during crises or disasters such as the 9/11 terrorist attack in 2001 or natural disasters such as Hurricane Katrina.[3] Not much attention, on the other hand, has been paid to day-to-day supply-chain security. As supply chains reach around the globe, potential security concerns are present every day. The focus of this chapter will be on developing a framework for global supply-chain security. With this framework, the supply-chain manager can develop strategies and tactics for maintaining security in the global supply chain.

Supply-chain security has four dimensions:

1. Security of the product or service
2. Security of the information flows
3. Security of the money flows
4. Security of the logistics systems

This chapter will look at each dimension in turn, provide a description, and give examples both good and bad.

The Product or Service

Security of the *product* or *service* itself has several dimensions. Underlying all of them is the question customers (meaning each successive link in the supply chain) must ask continually: "Am I getting what I ordered or expected?" Pharmaceutical companies are particularly at risk. Pills are small, easily counterfeited, valuable, and easy to conceal. If the customer does not receive the genuine item, lives and the company's reputation are at risk. The more people who handle the drug before it reaches the consumer, the greater the risk of a security breach. According to the Pharmaceutical Security Institute, from 2000 through 2009, the number of seizures globally of counterfeit, illegally diverted, and stolen pharmaceuticals grew from about 200 to over 2,000. (Keep in mind that these are the shipments that were detected.) Over a third of the seizures in 2009 were in Asia. Pfizer Inc. reported that it "confirmed fake versions of its drugs in at least 75 countries, and in the legitimate supply chain in at least 25 countries."[4] In Europe alone, the so-called gray market for drugs (those obtained through illicit channels) is over €10 billion. Counterfeit drugs are estimated to kill at least 100,000 people per year.[5] Of the drugs in circulation globally, 30%–50% are fakes with a value of $45 billion.[6]

Tracking Products

Pharmaceutical companies, for example, have elaborate procedures to insure that cheap generics or even placebos are not substituted for high-value drugs at some point in the distribution system.[7] Their efforts are intended to insure that the end customer receives the medication that he or she is expecting. Oracle has developed tracking software to insure the integrity of the supply chain. IBM, 3M, and Abbott Laboratories have developed radio-frequency identification (RFID) tracking systems for drugs. Johnson & Johnson has developed verification software. A firm in Ghana has introduced a verification system based on validation codes and mobile phones.[8] PharmaSecure, a New Hampshire start-up company, has developed a similar system and introduced it in India, where most of their employees are located.[9]

Outside the pharmaceuticals industry, Walmart has taken the lead in tracking products with RFID technology. They expect to tag all their products in their more than 3,750 U.S. stores. RFID tags not only help control inventory and especially inventory "shrinkage" (loss by theft) but can insure that the items they put on the shelves are indeed genuine and not counterfeits.[10]

Specifications

A company may receive the products it ordered from a supplier, but the products may not be made to specifications. Stories of toys painted with lead-based paint from China have made for sensational headlines.[11] Again, people's health and lives as well as companies' reputations are at risk from such a security breach. Ironically, the lead in the paint came largely from recycled electronic goods shipped to China from the United States.[12] Drywall from China has turned out to be a health threat because of unpleasant odors.[13] Commercial products are not the only ones at risk. The defense supply chain has been contaminated with counterfeit, defective computer chips from China. The Department of Defense reported 115 such incidents between 2002 and 2008. Weapon systems from the F-15 fighter jet to the aircraft carrier USS *Ronald Reagan* have been affected.[14]

Quality

Products might not be made to the quality standards that have been specified or cheaper substitute raw materials or components might have been used. Products received could contain illegally obtained components through either outright theft or the theft of intellectual property. You may think you have an original product but find that you have a knockoff instead. Colgate warned consumers about authentic-looking tubes of their toothpaste that were labeled "Made in South Africa" (where Colgate does not manufacture toothpaste). The toothpaste was contaminated with diethylene glycol (DEG), the same poison found in Chinese toothpaste.[15] Or suppliers may simply cheat. One businessman told the author he had received a container full of rocks instead of steel from a Korean supplier. Each holiday season, reports appear of gift recipients finding rocks wrapped in Chinese newspapers in the boxes supposedly containing video devices.

Long Supply Chains

Sometimes the length or complexity of the supply chain makes security difficult. China accounts for 53.8% of U.S. imports of ginger. In July 2007, ginger contaminated with the pesticide aldicarb sulfoxide, a chemical that can cause adverse reactions in humans, was discovered in a California food store. The investigators uncovered seven links in the supply chain from the farmers in China to the retail store. Discovering the actual source of the contamination was virtually impossible since for any given shipment arriving in a food store, the links in the supply chain could be different each time.[16] Even in the highly regulated pharmaceutical industry, problems can arise with contaminated products. Shipments of Heparin from China, made from pig intestines and used in blood thinners, were contaminated.[17] Estimates of the number of deaths resulting from the contamination range from 3 to 80.[18] It took months to trace the source of the contamination. Heparin is not the only problem. The United States does not have the authority to regulate overseas suppliers of pharmaceuticals even though 80% of the active ingredients in U.S. drugs originate overseas.[19] Can one depend on international partners to insure the safety of the global supply chain? The U.S. Food and Drug Administration (FDA) reported that their investigation into the contaminated Heparin was "severely hampered" by the Chinese government and that the Chinese government had done no investigating itself.[20]

Services

The service industry is not exempt from security issues. Many companies have found themselves in trouble with the immigration authorities because their suppliers were using undocumented workers.[21] Or sometimes subcontractors will not have the skills they claim to have. Countries such as Germany with a long history of guilds are stricter about the licensing of service providers than is the United States. The United States has an array of licensing and bonding procedures to try to ensure integrity (but not necessarily competence) in the service supply chain, but these vary widely from locality to locality, and in fact, how often are credentials actually checked? The problem is exacerbated in global supply chains because the supply-chain manager may not even know what to ask for in the way of credentials.

The Customer

In addition to these upstream issues, downstream, the customer wants to feel secure that he or she is receiving the service expected. Often this may involve communication or miscommunication with no fraud involved. For example, anyone who has opened a bank account in another country knows the feeling of insecurity as to what exactly is involved. The Citizens Bank in New England (a subsidiary of the Royal Bank of Scotland) addressed this in Boston by printing their marketing materials and account information in Chinese. They wanted the large number of Chinese students in Boston universities to feel secure as customers in the supply chain.[22]

Information

Security of information flows is a persistent problem. Since much of the information these days flows by electronic means, the data must be protected from corruption, malicious altering, or theft. Fortunately, electronic transactions are now so ubiquitous that this problem is being worked on constantly, although with varying degrees of success. In global supply chains, there are so many issues other than security related to information flows—such as timing, measurement systems, language, and so on—that security is often a relatively low priority. As a result, one hears stories of customer information (which is processed in offshore facilities) being stolen and sold to competitors. Electronic information gathering is ubiquitous.[23] Information, however, is not always electronic. The *Boston Globe* wrapped its newspapers and those of a sister newspaper (both are owned by the New York Times Company) in papers containing the names and credit card information of 240,000 of their subscribers and left them on street corners (intended for the distributors) for anyone to pick up.[24]

From 2006 to 2007, the theft of personal data tripled. More than 162 million records were reported lost or stolen in 2007, most in the United States, where disclosure laws make it easier to track incidents. Arrests or prosecutions were reported in only 19 of these cases. The source of the losses ranged from schools, to private companies, to government agencies and health organizations.[25] A 2010 report by NetWitness disclosed that hackers had broken into the computer systems at 2,411 companies over 18 months, gaining access to a variety of information from credit card data to intellectual property.[26]

In addition to the problem of organizations failing to protect their data adequately, a major problem is that of employees not taking security seriously. Employees tend to value data according to the cost of the medium on which it is stored. For example, workers in the British tax agency sent (and lost) two computer disks (of nominal intrinsic value) through interoffice mail. The data on the disks had a street value of $2.5 billion.[27] To make things worse, the apology letter sent to the "victims" contained unnecessary confidential information. (They sent 25 million letters, which means that many of them did not get to the intended recipient.) A further review showed that data had been lost from the same office eight times since in the previous 2 years.[28]

The proliferation of laptop computers in organizations is increasing the problem of security. Laptops are routinely taken out of the office (exposing them to the risk of outright theft) and connected to the home organization's central computer through a variety of sources from home connections to Wi-Fi connections in hotels and airports (increasing the chances of the data being intercepted). Booz Allen Hamilton, for example, supplied most of its 20,000 employees with laptops. Parts of the U.S. Treasury Department have up to 80% notebook computers in their computer mix. Millions of laptops are lost or stolen every year; 1 in 20 is recovered. Eighty percent of businesses report losing one or more laptops with sensitive information yearly.[29] External threats are not the only problem. In the past 10 years, the IRS has opened 4,700 investigations into the illegal use of taxpayer information by its employees. The cases ranged from simple curiosity, to the sale of information to third parties, to blackmail and extortion.[30] IT shops are having to rethink how they maintain the security of their hardware and the data contained in their machines in an environment in which it is increasingly easy to lose the data through theft or negligence.

Protecting Data

The primary methods of electronic data protection are passwords and PINs. Both are subject to an array of problems ranging from forgetting and sharing to outright theft. A recent poll in the United States, for example, found that the most commonly used password is "password."[31] More-advanced biometric methods, such as fingerprints and retina scans, have a higher degree of security but require specialized (and relatively expensive) equipment.[32] The most recent development that shows great promise is the methodology requiring the user to type in a string of characters (such as a sentence). This is matched with a profile the user has entered earlier. If there is a match, the user is allowed access to the system. The Psylock method developed in Germany is based on 17 different biometric parameters.[33] It cannot be shared with others because the user cannot verbalize the parameters. Psylock can even do ordinary tasks such as resetting passwords to avoid the practice of stealing passwords by falsely requesting a new one.[34] In addition to its high degree of security and simplicity, the other advantages are that it requires no specialized equipment and works anywhere there is a connection back to the central computer.

Money

Security of *money flows* is often mixed in with information flows. A prime example of this is credit cards. The use of credit cards exposes the users (both payer and payee) to the risk of the payment being diverted. Additionally, the use of credit cards exposes the payee to the risk that the personal data required to complete the transaction will be stolen and used to make purchases without the owner's knowledge or even used to steal the owner's identity. The largest publicized case of this happening recently is the 2007 TJX security breach. Through poor security measures, TJX exposed at least 45.7 million credit-card users to loss of personal information. The encryption protocol at TJX was weaker than that recommended for home Wi-Fi systems, and TJX retained the data too long (increasing the probability of a security breach).[35] Even if none of the data is used illegally, there is a significant cost to the banks, which must reissue credit cards to their customers at a cost of around $20 per card. TJX agreed to pay Visa and its banks up to $49.5 million to cover these costs.[36] For a relatively small investment in better security measures, management could have avoided not only the payment to Visa but also the continuing bad publicity. Unfortunately, in global commerce, security breaches such as the one at TJX have become commonplace as data thieves continue to improve their methods faster than companies install methods to protect themselves. The 2011 Epsilon

Data Management LLC security breach by hackers resulted in the loss of customer identification data by a number of large U.S. firms, including Kroger, J. P. Morgan, Chase, Walgreens, and Marriott.[37] Other significant data breaches involving personal information and credit card information have been Heartland Payment Systems (2009), Sony (2011), the National Archives and Records Administration (2009), and the U.S. Department of Veterans Affairs (2006). No one, it seems, is immune to electronic theft of data.[38]

Elaborate systems have evolved to protect both the buyer and the seller in international commerce. Devices such as letters of credit and contract protocols were developed in an age when communication was by written document or telex and funds were transferred from bank to bank as a result of manual instructions from bank employees. In the electronic age, individuals are able to make transfers around the world from their banks to virtually any other banks. This ease of access to the system means there is a greater chance of misdirected transactions, lost transactions, or fraudulent transactions. Letters of credit and contract protocols are still important but are not guarantees of security. Both the buyers and sellers must have confidence that they will receive their goods and payments if a system of international commerce is to work.

The problem of money security is becoming exacerbated as more non-traditional organizations function as banks. In parts of the developing world, for example, the mobile phone companies are performing functions, such as transferring funds, that are traditionally done by banks. At times, even the medium of exchange is mobile-phone minutes.[39] As funds flow through media such as mobile-phone networks instead of traditional channels, security of money flows becomes an increasing problem. For the global supply-chain manager, this phenomenon is not just a curiosity; it is one he or she must be prepared to deal with to insure security of money flows.

Supply chains do not always operate within the legal system. The flow of drugs from South America to the United States is through a complex, well-organized supply chain. To keep the flow of money back to Columbia secure, the organizations have begun using the legitimate banking system. They hire teams of workers to take bundles of cash to automatic teller machines (ATMs) in New York, making small deposits in each to avoid detection by the system. The organization then uses the ATMs in Columbia to withdraw the funds.[40] This avoids the problem of having to carry large amounts of cash out of the United States (which must be reported) or engaging in complicated laundering operations. In other words, they have found a secure method of letting their money flow through the supply chain. Legitimate businesses would benefit from being half as clever as those operating illegally.

The Logistics System

Security of the *logistics system* is becoming ever more important. The most blatant of the problems is piracy. In addition to normal commerce, relief organizations are affected. A ship with relief supplies for Somalia, for example, never left the port in Kenya after being warned of pirates.[41] Vacationers face the same risks. A French cruise ship and multiple private yachts have been seized by pirates in the same region. Despite the efforts of multiple governments, piracy off the shores of Somalia continues to be highly profitable for the pirates. Piracy is also common in the narrow straits between Singapore and the Philippines. Many heavily traveled shipping routes pass through areas where war or violence is common or a threat. Examples are the Strait of Hormuz between Iran and Oman (a major passageway for petroleum) or the Horn of Africa (at the southern exit to the Suez Canal). Ninety-five percent of the world's trade, valued at $6 trillion in 2007, travels by water. The annual cost of piracy is estimated to be between $3.5 and 8 billion.[42] "Ships and their crews disappear on the high seas and coastal waters every year, never to be seen again." The problem is bad enough that the International Maritime Bureau has established a piracy reporting and rescue center in Kuala Lumpur. The U.S. Navy is active in responding to calls for help both directly and through the center.[43] Because of the threat of terrorism in the logistics system, the U.S. Department of Homeland Security has formed the Customs-Trade Partnership Against Terrorism (C-TPAT). They provide statistics, suggestions, guidelines, and procedures regarding risk in the logistics system. For example, in a 2009 study of security breaches, they found the following:

34%	Conveyance Security: Conveyances not inspected
35%	Business Partner Requirements: Failure to Screen Business Partners
41%	Instruments of International Traffic (containers, trailers, pallets, etc.) not secured/properly inspected prior to loading
44%	Seal Controls: Lack of Seal Procedures
53%	Transportation Monitoring: Inadequate transportation Monitoring
68%	Security Procedures not followed (lack of checks, balances, accountability)[44]

In other words, the firms involved were not following even the most basic of precautions for protecting their shipments.

Ship Sizes

Another change that is causing increasing security problems is the size of ships. Larger ships are unable or have difficulty navigating traditional shipping routes. Ships that cannot go through the Panama Canal (opened in 1914 with locks to accommodate the ships of that era), for example, must go around Cape Horn or through the Strait of Magellan, both treacherous. (Panama is currently widening the locks in the canal.) Ships sailing from the U.S. West Coast or Canada to Asia travel a great circle route through the Aleutian Islands, again treacherous. Or the East Indies, in addition to harboring pirates, have waters that are shallow and passages that are narrow. Larger ships also run the risk of losing more cargo if there is an accident. Examples are oil spills from running aground or containers falling off ships. Estimates of the number of containers that fall off ships each year range from 2,000 to 10,000. An example so well known that it appeared in Ripley's Believe It or Not happened in 1992, when one container full of 28,800 bathtub toys fell off a ship in the Pacific Ocean.[45] Oceanographers have used the toys to track ocean currents. Some of the toys actually floated to the Atlantic Ocean.

The basic problem seems to be that shippers consider only the economies of scale in increasingly larger ships. If they considered the trade-off between size and security, they might prefer smaller ships, which are less at risk from treacherous waters because they draw less water and less at risk from pirates because they are faster and more maneuverable.

Another alternative for larger ships is to avoid routes such as the Panama Canal altogether. For example, containers may be off-loaded on one side of Panama and transported to the other side, where they can be reloaded on another ship; or they may be transported across the United States by train. On the other hand, this involves additional handling, which implies greater cost, security risk of loss, or risk of damage.

Summary

All supply chains, internal or external, domestic or global, have four dimensions of security. As supply chains expand around the globe and firms know less about their suppliers and customers and have less contact with them, the supply-chain manager must be aware of these security dimensions and devise ways of managing them. Overlooking any one of these dimensions can result in anything from a minor inconvenience to injury or death. How deeply into the supply chain one should exercise some control is a real question. The just-in-time philosophy, for example, says that a firm should trust its suppliers. The appropriate level of trust for a supplier in the same town or country, however, may not be appropriate for one halfway around the world. Should a firm care if its container is traveling around the Cape of Good Hope or going through the Suez Canal as long as it arrives when promised? Or should it be involved in these day-to-day decisions? What is the cost if your cargo is captured by pirates?

In the *Wall Street Journal*, Mark Vandenbosch and Stephen Sapp provide a four-point checklist for managing a global supply chain:

- Constantly monitor potential risks from suppliers.
- Make suppliers responsible and accountable.
- Change the ways you test and measure to be more appropriate in the global arena.
- Use government and industry regulation where it will reduce risk.[46]

With the framework of the dimensions of supply-chain security, an organization can divide its security concerns into manageable units and organize its efforts to protect itself, its customers, and its suppliers. In today's global supply chains, not doing so amounts virtually to gross negligence. Take actions to protect yourself:

- Use existing mechanisms to protect yourself against product and payment fraud. Examples are letters of credit and trade protocols in contracts.
- Use tracking systems such as those involving RFID chips to ensure that the goods you order or ship are the goods that arrive.
- Secure your financial transactions.
  - Do not rely on passwords!
  - Use biometric security methods.
- Treat information and the media on which it is stored as you would any other valuable asset. Protect it, encrypt it, and limit access to it.
- Assess the risks in your logistics system, assign costs to those risks, and take measures to mitigate against them. Use resources such as the C-TPAT 5 Step Risk Assessment Process Guide.[47]

CHAPTER 7

Day-to-Day Issues

Having a good broad-based background in global supply chains is helpful to the supply-chain manager, but there are also day-to-day issues with which the manager must deal constantly. Some of these issues can be found in the differences between domestic and global supply chains. A good starting point is the list of seven wastes in lean systems found in chapter 4. All are important issues in both domestic and global supply chains, but there are significant differences among them. Beyond the so-called wastes are additional issues such as outsourcing versus insourcing, the role of costs, and issues that may have completely different dimensions in the global arena.

The Seven Wastes

Rather than go back over all seven of the wastes, here we shall look at the most important issues relating to the wastes that arise in the management of global supply chains.

Transportation

The first difference between domestic and global supply chains is distance or transportation. As noted earlier, it takes 21 days to export a container from China. When this is added to the transit time over the Pacific, it takes on average 45 days to receive a container from China.[1] There are valid reasons for trying to reduce transportation time, many of which are negated in global commerce. One problem is the risk of not getting what you ordered—either the wrong product or the wrong level of quality. If this happened domestically, you could call your supplier and get a reshipment within days; globally it may take months. Another downside of global supply chains, as pointed out earlier, is the cost of carrying the pipeline inventory. A third is the risk of loss. A fourth is the risk of design changes while the shipment is en route. As Pete Engardio points out in *Business Week*,

> [One] might be able to buy a harness from China for 15% less than in Mexico. But if a design is altered after a batch of Chinese-made harnesses is already on the boat from Shanghai, the company has to foot the bill for up to six weeks of shipping and handling of obsolete parts.[2]

Excess Production

Excess production is another potential waste. Excess production can be, among other things, the result of poor scheduling, poor forecasting, or inappropriate lot sizes. All these are likely to occur in global supply chains. Forecasting is difficult because of long lead times required to place orders from abroad. The inaccurate forecast might have an impact on scheduling, or the manager might simply have lost control of the scheduling process. Inappropriate lot sizes may result from the need to fill a container or other shipping unit from abroad. All these can be managed well domestically but are difficult to control in a global supply chain.

Quality

Another waste is producing goods that do not meet quality standards. Producing abroad does not intrinsically mean poor quality, but it does mean less control over quality at the source. Unless one has quality personnel on site, it is the vendor who will have total control over quality. Volkswagen is noted for having its own quality people on site at vendors' overseas facilities. Smaller firms do not have this option and have to rely on the promises of their contractors. Quality control is often reduced to inspecting the finished product only after it has been received, a practice that has been discredited since the beginnings of the total quality management (TQM) movement in the 1980s. It is important for the supply-chain manager not to apply blanket judgments to countries or areas. Several supply-chain managers have told the author that they prefer production in China to Mexico, despite the difference in distance, because the quality is better. This, of course, can vary widely from firm to firm.

Maintaining Schedules

Maintaining schedules is perhaps the most difficult aspect of being in a global supply chain. Lean management teaches us that shortening the throughput time leads to multiple benefits, including the following:

- More flexible responses to customers
- Faster responses to engineering changes
- Increased capacity
- Reduced cash cycle time
- Faster response to quality problems
- More accurate forecasting
- Better on-time completion and delivery times

Being part of a global supply chain can negate all these benefits. Many of the points have been touched on previously, but it is helpful to bring them together in the context of production scheduling. The ideal production schedule will result in exactly what the customer wants, when he wants it, where he wants it, and at the price and level of quality he wants. Outsourcing and being part of a global supply chain is generally believed to result in lower costs and thus the price the customer wants.

The Ohio Art case used earlier is a perfect example of many of the benefits of short throughput times being negated in global supply chains. Ohio Art had to deliver the Etch A Sketch toy to their customers—Walmart, Target, and Toys "R" Us—at a price that would allow the customers to sell it for under $10. Production in China appeared to Ohio Art to be the only solution. Production had to be scheduled in the spring for fall delivery (for the December holiday season).

Because of transportation time, there was no opportunity to make changes to the production plan. If the toy somehow became a fad (e.g., it was featured in the most popular Dilbert cartoon of all time),[3] there would be no opportunity to increase production at the last minute.

Conversely, if it were somehow labeled a health threat, there would be little time to cancel the order. Quality and engineering response times would be lengthened, and the cash cycle time would be longer. Another example is Sauder Furniture. They had a customer response time goal of 4 days, yet their supply line to their overseas vendors was 3 months.[4]

Excess Inventory

As pointed out earlier, these problems are mitigated by carrying more inventory. It is a case of the classic "water and rocks" analogy in reverse. The analogy was introduced in the early 1980s by Robert Hall during the APICS (American Production and Inventory Management Society) Zero Inventories Crusade.[5] The water was inventory and the rocks were problems, particularly scheduling problems or poor scheduling practices. The problems and practices could be corrected by gradually lowering the level of the water (inventory) and exposing the rocks (problems and practices) one at a time. Each would be fixed and the water would be lowered again. Now, in the era of global supply chains, the problems have been reintroduced, so inventory levels are increased to hide them.

To Outsource or Not?

The ultimate question is, "Should a firm outsource abroad?" There are many arguments in favor of the practice. Producing abroad allows one to be closer to overseas markets and thus more easily tailor products and services to the local customers. Producing in other countries moves one behind tariff and quota barriers. Likewise, much transaction risk in foreign exchange can be avoided by dealing in fewer currencies. A firm can increase capacity without investing in facilities or equipment. BMW, for example, in 2003 outsourced the design and production of their X3 compact sport-utility vehicle to Magna Steyr, an Austrian firm. Magna had already produced cars for Mercedes-Benz, Audi, Volkswagen, Jeep, and Chrysler. By outsourcing, BMW was able to get the new model to market more quickly without a large investment in capital and labor.[6] The key is "right-sourcing"—outsourcing the right products and processes to the right place with the right partner that will return maximum value for the enterprise.[7]

Local Talents

Outsourcing abroad allows one to take advantage of local talents. The Germans pride themselves on engineering and the Indians pride themselves on their IT skills. There are large labor pools of U.S.-educated, English-speaking engineers, computer scientists, and even lawyers in the Philippines and India (typically earning lower salaries than their American counterparts). The author knew of an unemployed IT engineer in the United States who asked a friend of his (who was a supervisor in an IT firm) if there were any jobs available. She replied that everyone who worked for her was in India. The suggestion that the American move to India to find a job was not met favorably. He became a dance instructor instead. This type of outsourcing arrangement is made possible, of course, by the rapid advances in communications technology. It is now possible for a manager to observe and check on the work of subordinates around the globe. Some firms exploit this capability by passing work around the globe so that work is being done 24/7. Peter Frykman, the founder of Driptech Inc., commented that "thanks to the revolution in communications technology he is able to hand off work in the evening to his co-workers in Asia, and pick it back up in the morning. 'If you get the rhythm right, you can really be working around the clock as an organization,' he says."[8]

Economies of Scale

Becoming a global firm allows a company to achieve economies of scale. Controlling all operations worldwide can eliminate the overhead associated with having a headquarters in each country or area of the world. If the firm gets too large, this can lead to span-of-control problems. Span-of-control problems are exacerbated in the global economy by the issues raised earlier—culture, time, language, distance, and so on.

Insourcing

Some companies that have done significant amounts of outsourcing are beginning to reverse the process (so-called insourcing or onshoring). Apple has begun to move its design process in-house to protect its intellectual property: "[Apple] executives have expressed concern that some information shared with outside vendors could find its way into chips sold to Apple competitors," and "[Steve Jobs] wanted to develop chips internally and didn't want knowledge about the technology to leave Apple."[9] Sharp's newest LCD factory in Sakai, Japan, has a campus containing all their major vendors—no shipping, no loss of intellectual property.[10]

Spanish clothing chain Zara, which has stores in Europe and the United States, keeps ahead of its rivals by maintaining "an iron grip on every link in its supply chain." Instead of producing fashion products in Asia, where costs are lower, its production facilities are in Spain, Portugal, and North Africa. The result is higher costs but faster response to changing demand (2 weeks instead of up to 6 months), faster deliveries (24–48 hours), and better forecasting and production scheduling (which eliminates year-end sales of excess stock).[11]

United States apparel firms are learning the same lessons. The Los Angeles based women's clothing manufacturer Karen Kane is moving 80% of their production from China to Southern California. Michael Kane said that "declining production quality [and] unreliable shipping times" influenced the company's decision. Ilse Metchek, president of the California Fashion Association, is quoted as saying, "Fashion changes every 10 weeks. You cannot keep up with that if you are producing ten of thousands of units in China."[12] Caterpillar and other large manufacturers are moving overseas production to U.S. facilities. The "companies are seeing disadvantages of offshore production, including shipping costs, complicated logistics, and quality issues. Political unrest and theft of intellectual property pose additional risks." General Electric is moving production of water heaters from China to Kentucky. Block Windows is moving production from China to Florida. "When we [looked] at the costs and complexities of the inventory and lead times, there really wasn't any savings," said president Roger Murphy.[13]

Some smaller companies are following the same path. In an article about northwest Ohio, the *Toledo Business Journal* summed up the problem this way:

Costly problems with product quality from foreign suppliers, the low value of the U.S. dollar versus other currencies, long shipping delays, increasing logistics costs, inventory carrying costs, and the difficulty of working with foreign suppliers are combining to cause some manufacturers to move parts and components sourcing back to northwest Ohio and southeast Michigan.[14]

These are exactly the same problems mentioned earlier. The problems are not all with Asia. A battery company moved its operations from Mexico back to Ohio:

In 2007, [Crown Battery] purchased a battery manufacturer in Reynosa, Mexico. The Mexican operations were experiencing high levels of quality issues and product returns due, in part, to high employee turnover. Crown Battery made the decision to close the Reynosa plant and move its production to Fremont, Ohio. "We found that our people in Fremont [could] actually produce a better battery than employees in Mexico that make $1.81 an hour," stated Hal Hawk, the company's president.[15]

Sauder Furniture, mentioned earlier, purchased 50% of certain parts needed to assemble its furniture from Asia. They decided that cost was not the only criterion they should use and that long supply chains were causing them difficulties: "In the past, we purchased these parts based solely on price. However, it is important to look at the bottom line cost to the business and not just purchase price." Sauder decided to shorten its supply chain to a within a maximum 250-mile (400-km) radius of their factory in Ohio and an ideal radius of 150 miles (240 km). It was willing to accept higher costs in exchange for offsetting the other problems associated with long supply chains.[16]

The memory-module producer Avant opened a new plant in Texas. According to the CEO, Tim Peddecord,

Manufacturing in the U.S allows Avant to turn around U.S. orders in 24 hours, an advantage in an industry where demand is so volatile and clients try to keep inventories low. In addition, the reduced freight costs, compared with shipping goods from China, can offset the added cost of U.S. labor.[17]

Decisions Based on Costs

It seems that most firms deciding to move into the global arena are driven by costs. Labor costs in many areas of the world are simply lower than they are in the developed countries. A social argument can be made for outsourcing on this basis. The workers accepting lower wages are actually making more than anyone in their families has ever made. Giving them jobs helps to raise their standard of living and break the cycle of poverty. On the other hand, the purpose of the firm is to provide value for the owners and stockholders by providing customers products and services they want, where they want them, when they want them, and at a price and level of quality they want. While costs are a valid basis for decision making, the shortcomings of the accounting system often make it difficult to make good decisions. In a study in 2005 by Deloitte & Touche, 44% of the companies surveyed said they did not cut costs by outsourcing globally, and more than half said they incurred costs not specified in their contracts with overseas vendors:[18]

> Cost is usually the major driver in a company's decision to purchase parts and products from abroad. Yet in a 2008 PricewaterhouseCoopers survey of retail and consumer-goods companies, one-quarter of respondents said they could not quantify actual savings. Many tracked transportation, customs, and warehousing costs. But quality and reliability of vendors often went unmeasured.[19]

In other words, the accounting system does not measure explicitly many of the costs that are important in global sourcing (or normal operations management, for that matter).

The cost of carrying inventory, for example, does not appear in the income statement. Its components may appear in different parts of the statement (taxes, warehousing, insurance, etc.), but the critical number of how much it costs to carry inventory is simply not there. The costs of quality (with the exception of warranty costs) are scattered throughout the company's accounts. The costs of inflexibility and nonresponsiveness are nowhere to be found. The cost of incurring additional risk because of long supply chains, additional handling, poor communications, late deliveries, and so on are difficult to measure but are real. Supply-chain and operations managers often use surrogate measures to compensate for this lack of accounting information. In one company visited by the author, when they received bids from vendors, they would estimate the probability of the risk factors just described and calculate the amount of safety stock necessary to protect against these risks. They then added the cost of this additional safety stock to the potential vendors' bids before making a decision.

Drivers of Hidden Costs

Phanish Puranam and Kannan Srikanth[20] describe three drivers of hidden costs in outsourcing—contracting, transition, and interaction—with some prescriptions (and some additional comments and prescriptions by the author).

Contracting

The first is contracting. If performance metrics for the processes are difficult to define and spell out, then one must take extra measures of due diligence to reassure oneself that the vendors will be able to perform as they promise and as you expect. A supply-chain manager described this process to the author. He had two bids for manufacturing a subassembly—one from China and one from Korea. They were virtually identical on paper except for cost—the Chinese bid was lower. He personally visited both companies and decided to award the contract to the Korean company, even though the Chinese company bid significantly lower. The key is that he made a personal visit to both companies. His decision was based on what he saw: the layouts of the factory floors, the offices of the managers and engineers, the warehousing systems, and the attitudes of the workers. It would be difficult to quantify these factors, but they have the potential to add significantly to bottom-line costs.

Are the skills required of the vendor generic or company specific? If they are not generic, the process may require more time on the part of your quality, engineering, and production people than you anticipated (including extensive [and expensive] travel to and from the vendor's site). If the skills required are specialized enough, vertical integration may be a better approach. If nothing else, having the function performed in-house (even though the "house" may be in another country) gives better protection for intellectual property.

A quality manager, Michael Rude, related an incident in his company to the author. He worked for a firm with an assembly operation in the United States. The purchasing department decided to outsource fabrication of the parts (a forging operation) to a Chinese company "based on a brochure and a salesman's presentation." Twenty percent of the first batch of parts they received from China were defective (and more were on the way). Mr. Rude's boss dispatched him immediately to China to find the problem. The airplane ticket alone cost the company $8,000 because it was purchased on short notice. When Mr. Rude arrived at the Chinese plant, he found it looked just like the brochure—except for the final step in the process. Workers were visually inspecting the parts and sorting them by "accept" and "reject." Fifty percent of the parts went in the reject pile. Of the 50% in the "accept" area, 20% were rejects by the U.S. company's standards. He finished by saying that someone should have visited the vendor before they signed the contract, not after container loads of defective parts started arriving in the United States with more on the way.[21]

Transition

The second area Puranam and Srikanth describe is transition. Are you sure the vendor is prepared to carry out the work? Are the documents describing your products and processes current, and are they translated if the vendor is in another country? Are they online so that all sites have the latest versions? When BMW outsourced the building of their new SUV to Magna Steyr, the contract was more than 5,000 pages long![22] Are the vendor's employees prepared to execute your process and make your product successfully? Will they need training? How much? What will it cost? Once you train them, will they stay? Or will turnover require continuous intensive training? If your vendor is in an area that is relatively new to manufacturing, do the employees have basic skills such as coming to work on time and staying for an entire shift? Are they local employees, or do they commute from long distances and thus are more likely to leave their jobs and return home or stay home after holiday visits?

Interaction

The third factor Puranam and Srikanth describe is interaction. Basically, where within the supply chain is the vendor, and how tightly linked is the vendor with other links in the thread? Is the linkage so tight that it will require constant communication, either electronically or in person? Are you prepared to deal with the time, language, and cultural elements of this communication? If the vendor fails to meet the performance metrics in terms of time, quantity, and quality, what will be the impact on the other links in the chain? Will you need to build extra safety stock (with its cost) into the system to protect against the risks?

Failure to consider and prepare for these drivers of cost leads to the situations described in the Deloitte & Touche and Pricewaterhouse-Coopers reports. Few if any of them appear explicitly in the accounting statements. Kripalani described five offshoring best practices.[23] The one most relevant here is the following: "Be prepared to invest time and effort." The CFO of Penske admitted, "It took a heck of a lot more involvement on the part of myself and my team than I expected."[24] Of course, time is money, which is additional cost. Penske invests heavily in training, including their processes and even English-language training to facilitate communication. According to a director of Gartner Research, "What's often lacking in offshore partners 'is a lot of deep process knowl-edge.'"[25] Things taken for granted in domestic employees may be totally outside the experience of employees in other countries. Processing insur-ance applications, for example, may be mystifying to someone who has never had nor ever heard of insurance.

New Areas of Management

Finally, managing a global supply chain may introduce new areas of management one normally does not encounter domestically. One is transportation. Although companies must manage their transportation domestically, there are many second-, third-, and fourth-tier logistics pro-viders who will manage the details. This can also be true globally, but the global transportation manager may be confronted with entirely new issues. Most global transportation of goods is by water. Ocean transpor-tation is far cheaper than other modes, especially since the only viable alternative is air transportation. For other than bulk goods, ocean movement involves containers. The following are some of the issues faced by the global supply-chain manager:

- How do I "stuff" my containers to improve efficiency and reduce the number of containers I need? A good stuffing algorithm can reduce the number of containers by up to 15%.
- Through which ports do I bring in my goods? Ports in western Canada are actually closer to Asia than ports in California. What is the infrastructure connecting the port to my facility or customers?
- Should I use only full containers or should I share containers and risk having my shipment held up by the customs service because of someone else's goods in the same container?
- What do I do with empty containers? Shipping empty containers is the same thing as "deadheading." It generates costs but no revenues.
- What ocean routes do I take to avoid pirates?
- What do I do if the borders are closed (e.g., September 11, 2001) or if the longshoremen go on strike?

Air transportation is much faster and more expensive, but it involves many of the same issues. Pirates are not a problem with air transportation, but natural events such as volcano eruptions can interrupt the flow of parts and goods. The eruption of Eyjafjallajökull in Iceland in 2010 caused the cancellation of 100,000 flights.

Transportation is not the only issue. Political risk became almost a forgotten issue in the 1990s. The new century has brought the problem back to the surface with a vengeance. What if our facility in another country is nationalized by the government (such as Libbey Glass in Venezuela)? Is it a critical link in our supply chain, or do I have alternatives? Chrysler, for example, built a factory in Peru that produced only half the parts needed to assemble a car. Had it been nationalized, it would have been worthless. What if there is political unrest in popular outsourcing sites, such as Thailand and Tunisia, or in regimes thought to be stable, such as Egypt and Libya? Is China as stable as we think? What if there is a war among drug gangs as seen along the border in Mexico, where the maquiladoras are located? What if the government begins inflating the money supply and causes hyperinflation (such as happened in Zimbabwe)? Countries in emerging markets "are rife with political risks—weak legal systems, makeshift infrastructure, volatile cities and weak regimes."[26] The wise firm involved in global supply chains will assess the overseas situation, do a risk analysis, and prepare contingency plans. The wise firm domestically will do the same, but the issues may be quite different.

Summary

Keep the following in mind when you are managing or preparing to manage a global supply chain:

- Know your costs and their impacts—even the costs that do not show up in the accounting statements.
- Assess your risks and develop measures to mitigate them. If you have business interruption insurance, check to see if it covers interruptions because of breaks in your supply chain.
- Know your vendors and your customers well *before* you start doing business with them.
- Be aware of all the decisions you will have to make; don't get caught by surprise.
- Be prepared to devote more time than you ever imagined would be necessary.
- Outsource because it makes good business sense, not because everyone else is doing it.

CHAPTER 8

Doing It Right

A Mini Case Study

Throughout this book, I have emphasized the problems and pitfalls of global supply chains. Although there are many problems and pitfalls, there can be significant benefits from producing abroad or using overseas sources. This final mini case study describes how a company, First Solar, has approached overseas expansion. They have, to date, been successful in these efforts. The following information is based on the public record[1] and discussions with members of their management team.

First Solar has been the leading solar panel company in the world. It was formed in 1999 and began production in 2002. It was founded in the Toledo, Ohio, area and still maintains its only U.S. production facility in Perrysburg, Ohio. Their corporate headquarters are in Tempe, Arizona. In 2008, they were the first solar panel company to reduce their production costs below $1 per watt. The market for solar panels is currently heavily dependent on governmental subsidies for solar power production, so this adds a level of uncertainty against which the company must hedge. First Solar has a 50-year warranty on their solar panels (specifically, they warrant that the panels will yield 80% or more of their design wattage for 50 years). In addition, they put aside funds from every panel sold to pay for recycling that panel when the customer has finished with it.

Overseas Locations

First Solar has eight production facilities, including overseas locations in Malaysia and Germany, with additional sites planned in Arizona, France, and Vietnam. They had a variety of reasons for producing overseas. The primary motivation for their move to Malaysia was labor cost. Although the production of solar panels is not particularly labor intensive, the competition is intense, and the small difference in labor costs was significant. In addition, the Asian market is growing, so they are closer to their customers.

They also have a factory in Frankfurt am Oder, Germany, near the German-Polish border. Although northern Germany would seem to be an unlikely site for solar power, there were two primary reasons for locating there. The first, as we mentioned before, was government subsidies. The Germans have a goal of eliminating their dependence on coal-fired and nuclear energy. Solar is one part of the mix. Second, during the cold war, the Soviet Union had a large military base near Frankfurt. A German businessman who was on the team to integrate the East and West German economies after 1991 told the author that the Russians had simply poured waste petroleum products on the ground to the extent that the soil was poisoned 20 meters deep. The only thing that can be done safely with such a site is to cover it, so the Germans decided to cover it with solar panels. First Solar was selected to produce the panels. In addition, with the high unemployment in the eastern German states, there was a readily available supply of skilled labor. Sixty-five percent of their sales in 2009 were in Germany.

First Solar is currently planning on expanding into Vietnam and has signed an agreement with China Power International New Energy Holding Ltd.[2] Vietnam is attractive because its labor costs are even lower than Malaysia's. Economic problems, including persistent inflation, have made it less attractive, however. China is a growing market for solar power, and the Chinese policy is to encourage or even require firms to produce in China what they sell in China. On the other hand, China has had problems protecting intellectual property. Since the production process is proprietary and a competitive advantage for First Solar, they had to assess the risk of compromising their intellectual property against the potential return from entering the large and growing Chinese market. At one time, they considered expanding into Thailand, but the political unrest there caused them to shelve those plans.

Transportation

One factor that is not significant in their location decisions is transportation costs. The cost of transporting their raw materials is about the same as transporting the solar panels. So they can choose to be close to either their customers or their suppliers based on other factors (such as currency risk).

Culture and Language

Wherever they open facilities, they are sensitive to the nuances of opening facilities in different cultures. Everyone at the company involved in opening and operating the new facilities abroad must undergo cultural training. They have contracted with universities to provide this training. In addition, local managers in the countries where they are expanding are brought to the United States to meet the people with whom they will be working and to learn the corporate culture. English is the mandated corporate language, but all operational documents, including shop-floor manuals, are translated into the local languages.

Part of their quality control system also aids in dealing with the potential problems of cultural differences. The system, called "Copy Smart," is designed to ensure that the production system is identical in every facility, whether in the United States or abroad. They do not want their customers preferring the panels from one facility over others. Although the primary purpose of the system is to ensure consistent quality worldwide, it also means that a manager may be assigned to any facility and find an identical layout and identical production processes. All workers, no matter what their nationalities, are given the same training and follow the same procedures. In theory, any worker could be placed in any production facility in the world and feel comfortable with the layout and environment.

Exchange-Rate Risk

Because they operate in multiple countries, they face exchange-rate risk. When asked how they deal with the risk, the answer they give is hedge, hedge, hedge! They have a department that specializes in managing currency risk. They also manage the risk by producing in countries where they sell their product. Producing in Germany, where they have 65% of their sales, means both their costs and their sales are in euros. They are also opening a new factory in Arizona to meet demand from the California utilities rather than import the panels from their Asian facilities. The proposed factory in France is considered a strategic move but also is based partially on mitigation of exchange-rate risk. France does not emphasize solar power at the moment (they depend heavily on nuclear power), but they are in the euro zone; plus, having a plant in France gives First Solar a seat at the French equivalent of the Business Roundtable so that they have a voice in future decisions about solar power.

Role of Government

The two biggest risks faced by First Solar are regulatory and financial—both determined by governments. Internally they say they are one politician's vote away from going out of business. Because their product is based on cadmium telluride, a hazardous substance in its raw form, the handling, use, and even access is government regulated. In the form in which they use it, the compound is not hazardous. In addition, they have reduced the amount of the compound needed by over 99%. They must ensure that the governments where they operate can distinguish between the two forms of the compound and will allow them to operate. The recycling program also assures the governments that the cadmium telluride will be reclaimed by First Solar and not be discarded into the environment.

The financial risk stems from the subsidies governments give to the solar industry. Although First Solar receives no direct subsidies because it is in the solar industry, its customers receive subsidies and tax breaks for generating clean, renewable power. These subsidies can be removed at any time. The German government, for example, at the start of 2011 had reduced their subsidies by 25% from a year earlier.[3] One of First Solar's competitors, Xunlight, shut down virtually their entire operation because they lost a multimillion-dollar Italian contract—the government reduced the subsidy and the customer cancelled the order.[4] First Solar uses three strategies to mitigate this risk: The first is to diversify their customer base so that one contract cancellation does not have such a large impact on the company. The second is to continue to reduce the cost of production so that subsidies are less important to make generating power with their panels economical. The third is to invest in solar power generating facilities that use their panels to give them a voice in decision making.[5]

Supply Risk

A long-term risk may be the relative scarceness of tellurium. It is a by-product of refining metals such as copper. The major sources are the United States, Canada, Japan, and Peru, so the supply should be stable. Although there is a sufficient supply at present to support solar-panel production, a significant expansion of production may begin straining the supply chain. In Germany, for example, which is committed to producing clean power, less than 2% of power generation is from solar sources, so the potential to expand the market is great. There are untapped sources of tellurium, such as the refining of gold, lead, and coal, but extracting it from these sources will increase costs. There are also a number of competing uses for tellurium. The recycling program will eventually give First Solar an additional source of tellurium through reclaiming it from older panels. Although with the 50-year warranty, this would seem to be in the distant future, as the technology improves, customers may choose to return the older panels sooner. In any event, tellurium is and will continue to be a scarce metal.

The Future

Since solar panel production is a new industry and there are a lot of competitors with different ideas, First Solar wants to be sure they survive the inevitable industry shake-out and emerge as the major player in the industry. Demand for solar panels doubled last year to 17 gigawatts and is expected to grow to 21 gigawatts in 2011, so the potential for First Solar is there.[6] On the other hand, the volatility of their stock price reflects the uncertainty in the industry. Effective management of their global supply chains is a key element in their long-term survival strategy.

Notes

Chapter 1

1. Davidson, A. (2010).
2. A display featuring this industry can be seen in the Henry Ford Museum in Dearborn, Michigan.
3. Chadwin et al. (1990), p. 1.
4. See Williamson (1998, 2009).
5. Melish (1916), pp. 73–75; Kettell (1916), pp. 280–284.
6. Foreman (2011), pp. 155–174.
7. Bloom times (2011), p. 42.
8. Smith (1937), pp. 3–12.
9. Schumpeter (1954), p. 607.
10. "So much gained" (2009), p. 11.
11. Winchester (2008), p. 8–10.
12. Maylie (2011), p. B1.
13. Maylie (2011), p. B1.
14. *Economic report* (1956), p. 148.
15. Sanders (2009a), p. B1; Sanders (2009b), p. B2.
16. Winning and Lee (2011), p. B3.
17. Kane and Clark (2009), p. B1.

Chapter 2

1. Majima (1994), p. 25.
2. Orlicky (1975).
3. Greene (1987), p. 4.2.
4. Hall (1981).
5. Hall (1983).
6. Goldratt and Cox (1984).
7. Bennett (2011), p. B7.
8. Sanchanta (2011), p. B1.
9. Dowell (2011), p. B1.
10. Tsi and Clark (2009), p. B1.
11. Interview with James Craig, plant operations manager, March 31, 2011.

Chapter 3

1. Oliver and Webber (1982), pp. 63–75.
2. Maylie (2011), p. B1.
3. ARN (2011).
4. Vonderembse (2002) and conversations with the Modine plant manager.
5. Engardio (2006), pp. 50–58.
6. Handfield (2002), p. 6.
7. Walker (2002), p. 29.
8. Engardio (2001); Berinato (2001).
9. Zimmerman (2010), p. A3.
10. Kahn (2003).
11. Rothfield (2010), p. C3.
12. Moffett and Pearson (2011), p. B1.
13. Moffett (2011), p. B1.
14. Bussey (2011), p. B1.
15. "Is Wal-Mart" (2003), pp. 49–50.
16. "Is Wal-Mart" (2003), pp. 49–50.
17. Stoll (2005), p. A6.
18. Planning (2004).
19. Pope et al. (2004).

Chapter 4

1. Friedman (2006), p. 151.
2. "So much gained" (2009), p. 11.
3. Hill (2008), pp. 264–265.
4. Reedy (2011), p. A3.
5. Williamson (2011), p. A1; Berman (2011).
6. *Economist* (2010), p. 244.
7. "Genetically modified crops" (2011), p. 105.
8. Dawson and Dean (2011), p. A1.
9. See *Economist* (2010).
10. Schroeder et al. (2011), p. 137.
11. Engardio (2009), p. 55.
12. Trent and Roberts (2010), pp. 123–125.
13. Aeppel (2010), p. A1.
14. Dvorak (2009), p. A1.

Chapter 5

1. Light (2011), p. B7.

2. Hill (2008), p. 92.
3. "Swiss bank" (2011), p. G4.
4. Maltby (2010), p. B5.
5. Trent and Roberts (2010), ch. 5.
6. Lahart (2011), p. B1.
7. Hill (2008), pp. 123–153.
8. Wild et al. (2010), pp. 100–108.
9. Convention (1998).
10. Loftus and Holzer (2011), p. B4.
11. "Corruption eruption" (2010c), p. 73.
12. See Rotary (2011).
13. Standage (2009), p. 13.
14. Wonacott (2011a), p. B1.
15. World Bank (2010), pp. 18–23.
16. World Bank (2010), p. 63.
17. World Bank (2010), pp. 145–205.
18. Lahart (2011), p. B1.
19. Rowley and Hiroko (2009), p. 50. One yen is about one U.S. cent.
20. Reiter and Power (2004), p. A10.
21. Dvorak (2010), p. C1.
22. Curren and Van Hasselt (2011), p. B8.
23. "Big Mac" (2004), p. 71.
24. Arntzen (2010), p. 4.
25. Hookway and Poon (2011), p. A8.
26. Abelson (2011), p. B5.

Chapter 6

1. Hymowitz (2007), p. B1.
2. Napolitano (2011), p. A17.
3. Melnyk et al. (2005), p. 31.
4. Beck (2008), p. B1.
5. "Poison" (2010), p. 65.
6. Darnton and Hornblower (2011).
7. Zoellner (2007), p. 4.
8. "Poison" (2010), p. 66.
9. Lahart (2011), p. B1.
10. Bustillo (2010), p. A1.
11. Casey (2007), p. A3.
12. Fairclough (2007), p. B1.
13. Corkery (2009), p. A3.
14. Grow et al. (2008), pp. 33–37.

15. Birchall (2007), p. 23.
16. Zamiska and Kesmodel (2007), p. A1.
17. Fairclough and Burton (2008), p. A1.
18. Darnton and Hornblower (2011).
19. Beck (2008), p. B1.
20. Mundy (2010), p. A7.
21. "160 illegal aliens" (2007).
22. Lee (2007), p. D1.
23. Flynn (2007), pp. 4–6.
24. Gavin (2006), p. A1.
25. Acohido (2007), p. B1.
26. Gorman (2010), p. A3.
27. Worthen (2007), p. B3.
28. "Learning" (2007), p. 95.
29. Charney (2007), p. B4.
30. Herman (2007), p. D3.
31. "10 most common" (2008).
32. Pope and Bartmann (2010), pp. 137–138.
33. Bartman et. al. (2007), p. 2.
34. Bartmann and Wimmer (2007), p. 4.
35. Pereira (2007), p. B3.
36. Kerber (2007), p. C3.
37. Daniel and Sidel (2011), p. B3.
38. "An anonymous foe" (2011), p. 67.
39. Wonacott (2011b), p. C1.
40. Schoofs (2007), p. A1.
41. "Ship stays put" (2007), p. 7.
42. Hansen (2011), p. B3.
43. Raffaele (2007), p. 40.
44. Department of Homeland Security (2010), p. 7.
45. Carty (2006), p. B3.
46. Vandenbosch and Sapp (2010), p. R8.
47. See Department of Homeland Security (2010).

Chapter 7

1. Engardio (2009), p. 55.
2. Engardio (2009), p. 55.
3. Adams (2008), p. 234.
4. "Sauder" (2010), p. 1.
5. Hall (1983), p. 13.
6. Edmonson (2003), pp. 18–19.

7. The author first encountered the term "right-sourcing" in Dilbert, April 17, 2011.

8. Lahart (2011), p. B1.

9. Kane and Clark (2009), p. B1.

10. Wakabayashi (2009), p. B1.

11. Capell (2008), p. 66.

12. Slosson (2011).

13. Maher and Tita (2010), p. B1.

14. "Sauder" (2010), p. 1.

15. "Sauder" (2010), p. 1.

16. "Sauder" (2010), p. 1.

17. Whitehouse (2010), p. B1.

18. "Firms that outsource" (2005), p. 11.

19. Engardio (2009), p. 55.

20. Puranam and Srikanth (2007), p. R6.

21. Presentation to the University of Toledo APICS Chapter, January 24, 2011.

22. Edmonson (2003), pp. 18–19.

23. Kripalani (2006), p. 61.

24. Kripalani (2006), p. 61.

25. Kripalani (2006), p. 61.

26. "Beyond economics" (2011b), p. 75.

Chapter 8

1. First Solar (2011).

2. Spegele (2011), p. B5.

3. "Shining a light" (2011), p. 76.

4. Harrison (2011).

5. Eavis (2010), p. C12.

6. Spegele (2011), p. B5.

References

10 most common passwords. (2008, May 8). *PC Magazine*. Retrieved October 20, 2008, from http://www.pcmag.com/article2/0,1759,2113976,00.asp

160 illegal aliens arrested in Ohio raid. (2007, August 27). *Toledo Blade*.

Abelson, A. (2011, March 26). No exit, no entry. *Barron's*, B5.

Acohido, B. (2007, December 10). Theft of personal data more than triples this year. *USA Today*, B1.

Adams, S. (2008). *20 years of Dilbert*. Kansas City, MO: Andrews McMeel Publishing.

Aeppel, T. (2010, January 27). "Bullwhip" hits firms as growth snaps back. *Wall Street Journal*, A1.

An anonymous foe. (2011, June 18). *Economist*, 67–68.

ARN. (2011). Retrieved July 23, 2011, from http://www.arn.nl/english

Arntzen, B. (2010). *Global supply chain risk management part 2: Differences in frequencies and priorities*. Cambridge, MA: MIT Center for Transportation and Logistics.

A bank in every pocket? (2007, November 15). *Economist*. Retrieved June 19, 2011, from http://www.economist.com/node/10133998

Bartmann, D., Bakdi, I., & Achatz, M. (2007, April/June). On the design of an authentification system based on keystroke dynamics using a predefined input text. *International Journal of Information Security and Privacy*, *1* (2), 1–12.

Bartmann, D., & Wimmer, M. (2007). Kein problem mehr mit vergessenen passwoertern. *Datenschutz und Datenversicherheit*, *3*, 1–5.

Beck, M. (2008, April 8). Why you can't tell where your medication was made. *Wall Street Journal*, B1.

Bennett, J. (2011, March 31). Quake spurs supplier. *Wall Street Journal*, B7.

Berinato, S. (2001, August 1). What went wrong at Cisco in 2001. *CIO Newsletter*. Retrieved March 17, 2011, from http://www.cio.com/article/30413/What_Went_Wrong_at_Cisco_in_2001?page=2&taxonomyId=3154

Berman, J. (2011, March 4). U.S., Mexico focus on cross-border trucking compromise. *Logistics Management*. Retrieved June 17, 2011, from http://www.logisticsmgmt.com/article/u.s._mexico_focus_on_cross-border_trucking_compromise/

Beyond economics. (2011b, February 12). *Economist*, 75.

The Big Mac index: Food for thought. (2004, May 27). *Economist*, 71.

Birchall, J. (2007, June 15). Colgate toothpaste alert. *Financial Times*, 23.

Bloom times. (2011a, January 22). *Economist*, 42.

Bogart, E., & Thompson, C. (1916). *Readings in the economic history of the United States*. New York, NY: Longmans, Green and Co.

Bussey, J. (2011, March 9). Fear, distraction at Renault. *Wall Street Journal*, B1.

Bustillo, M. (2010, July 23). Wal-Mart radio tags to track clothing. *Wall Street Journal*, A1.

Capell, K. (2008, October 20). Zara thrives by breaking all the rules. *BusinessWeek*, 66.

Carty, S. S. (2006, August 4). When cargo gets lost at sea. *USA Today*, B3.

Casey, N. (2007, August 2). Mattel toys to be pulled amid lead fears. *Wall Street Journal*, A3.

Chadwin, M. L., Pope, J. A., & Talley, W. K. (1990). *Ocean container transportation*. New York, NY: Taylor & Francis.

Charney, B. (2007, December 18). Catching hold of computers set free. *Wall Street Journal*, B4.

Convention on Combating Bribery of Foreign Public Officials in International Business Transactions. (1998). Organisation for Economic Co-operation and Development. (DAFFE/IME/BR(97)20).

Corkery, M. (2009, January 12). Chinese drywall cited in building woes. *Wall Street Journal*, A3.

The corruption eruption. (2010c, May 1). *Economist*, 73.

Curren, D., & Van Hasselt, C. (2011, April 14). Loonie hinders Canadian firms. *Wall Street Journal*, B8.

Daniel, R., & Sidel, R. (2011, April 4). Breach at Epsilon exposes e-mails. *Wall Street Journal*, B3.

Darnton, K., & Hornblower, S. (producers). (2011, March 13). The fight against counterfeit drugs. *60 Minutes* Television Broadcast. New York, NY: CBS Broadcasting Inc.

Davidson, A. (2010). He shapes ship shapes by the sea shore. *This American Life*. Heard on Michigan Public Radio January 29, 2011. Originally aired January 22, 2010.

Dawson, C., & Dean, J. (2011, February 14). Rising China bests a shrinking Japan. *Wall Street Journal*, A1.

Department of Homeland Security. (2010). *C-TPAT 5 step risk assessment process guide*. http://www.cbp.gov/linkhandler/cgov/.../ctpat_assessment.../ctpat _assessment.pdf

Dowell, A. (2011, March 25). Japan: The business aftershocks. *Wall Street Journal*, B1.

Dvorak, P. (2009, May 18). Clarity is missing link in supply chain. *Wall Street Journal*, A1.

Dvorak, P. (2010, March 22). This time, Canada Inc. is set for dollar parity. *Wall Street Journal*, C1.

Eavis, P. (2010, March 22). First Solar flies too close to sun. *Wall Street Journal*, C12.

Economic report of the president. (1956). Washington, DC: Government Printing Office.

Economist. (2010). *Pocket world in figures.* London: Profile Books.

Edmonson, G. (2003, December 1). Look who's building Bimmers. *Business-Week*, 18–19.

Engardio, P. (2001, March 19). Why the supply chain broke down. *Business Week*, 41.

Engardio, P. (2006, January 30). The future of outsourcing. *Business Week*, 50–58.

Engardio, P. (2009, June 15). China's eroding advantage. *Business Week,* 54–55.

Fairclough, G. (2007, July 12). Lead toxins take a global round trip. *Wall Street Journal*, B1.

Fairclough, G., & Burton, T. M. (2008, February 21). The Heparin trail. *Wall Street Journal*, A1.

Firms that outsource report hidden costs. (2005, May 5). *Toledo Blade*, 11.

First Solar. (2011). Products. Retrieved April 1, 2011, from http://www.first solar.com/en/products.php

Flynn, S. (2007, September 16). Is anything private anymore? *Parade Magazine*, 4–6.

Foreman, A. (2011). *A world on fire: Britain's crucial role in the American Civil War.* New York, NY: Random House.

Friedman, T. (2006). *The world is flat.* New York, NY: Farrar, Straus and Giroux.

Gavin, R. (2006, February 1). Subscriber credit data distributed by mistake. *Boston Globe*, A1.

Genetically modified crops. (2011, February 26). *Economist*, 105.

Goldratt, E., & Cox, J. (1984). *The goal.* Croton-on-Hudson, NY: North River Press.

Gorman, S. (2010, February 18). Hackers mount new strike. *Wall Street Journal*, A3.

Greene, J. H. (Ed.). (1987). *Production and inventory control handbook*, New York, NY: McGraw Hill.

Grow, B., Tschang, C.-C., Edwards, C., & Burnsed, B. (2008, October 13). Dangerous fakes. *Business Week*, 33–44.

Hall, R. (1981). *Kawasaki, USA (1981).* Washington, DC: American Production and Inventory Control Society.

Hall, R. (1983). *Zero inventories.* Homewood, IL: Dow-Jones-Irwin.

Handfield, R. B., & Nichols, E. L. (2002). *Supply chain redesign.* Saddle River, NJ: Prentice-Hall.

Hansen, E. H. (2011, May 9). Piracy spurs Maersk to raise fee. *Wall Street Journal*, B3.

Harrison, S. (2011, April 12). Xunlight lays off 30 local workers after client fails to pay $5M order. *Toledo Blade*. Retrieved July 12, 2011, from http://www.toledoblade.com/business/2011/04/12/Xunlight-lays-off-30 -local-workers-after-client-fails-to-pay-5M-order.html

Herman, T. (2007, December 19). IRS combats in-house snoops. *Wall Street Journal*, D3.

Hill, C. W. L. (2008). *Global business today*. New York, NY: McGraw-Hill.

Hookway, J., & Poon, A. (2011, March 18). Crisis tests supply chain's weak links. *Wall Street Journal*, A8.

Hymowitz, C. (2007, August 27). Recent news events should have executives reviewing priorities. *Wall Street Journal*, B1.

Is Wal-Mart too powerful? (2003, October 6). *BusinessWeek*, 49–50.

Kahn, G. (2003, September 11). Made to measure: Invisible supplier has Penney's shirts all buttoned up. *Wall Street Journal*, C1.

Kane, Y., & Clark, D. (2009, April 30). In major shift, Apple builds its own team. *Wall Street Journal*, B1.

Kerber, R. (2007, December 21). NE banks, TJX reach agreement on breach. *Boston Globe*, C3.

Kettell, T. (1916). Eighty years' progress. In Bogart, E., & Thompson, C. (Eds.), *Readings in the economic history of the United States* (287–291). New York, NY: Longmans, Green and Co.

Kripalani, M. (2006, January 30). Five offshore practices that pay off. *BusinessWeek*, 61.

Lahart, J. (2011, January 27). For small businesses, the big world beckons. *Wall Street Journal*, B1.

Learning the embarrassing way. (2007, December 22). *Economist*, 95.

Lee, S. Y. (2007, September 11). Citizens court Chinese. *Boston Globe*, D1.

Light, J. (2011, January 18). Help wanted: Multilingual employees. *Wall Street Journal*, B7.

Loftus, P., & Holzer, J. (2011, April 9). J&J settlement in bribery case. *Wall Street Journal*, B4.

Maher, K., & Tita, B. (2010, March 12). Caterpillar joins "onshoring" trend. *Wall Street Journal*, B1.

Majima, I. (1994). *JIT: Kostensenkung durch just-in-time production*. Herbig, Germany: Wirtschaft Langen Müller.

Maltby, E. (2010, January 19). Expanding abroad? Avoid cultural gaffes. *Wall Street Journal*, B5.

Maylie, D. (2011, April 27). Firms seek supply route around conflict in Congo. *Wall Street Journal*, B1.

Melish, J. (1916). Travels through the United States of America. In Bogart, E., & Thompson, C. (Eds.), *Readings in the economic history of the United States* (285–287). New York, NY: Longmans, Green and Co.

Melnyk, S. A., Zsidisin, G. A., & Ragatz, G. L. (2005, November/December). The plan before the storm. *APICS Magazine*, 31.

Moffett, S. (2011, March 4). Renault concedes spy case doubts. *Wall Street Journal*, B1.

Moffett, S., & Pearson, D. (2011, January 7). Spying probe centers on electric cars. *Wall Street Journal*, B1.

Mundy, A. (2010, July 22). China never investigated tainted Heparin, probe says. *Wall Street Journal*, A7.

Napolitano, J. (2011, January 6). How to secure the global supply chain. *Wall Street Journal*, A17.

Oliver, R., & Webber, M. (1982). Supply-chain management: Logistics catches up with strategy. In M. Christopher (Ed.), *Logistics: The strategic issues* (pp. 63–75). London: Chapman and Hall.

Orlicky, J. (1975). *Material requirements planning*. New York, NY: McGraw-Hill.

Pereira, J. (2007, September 26). TJX's security system faulted in Canada probe. *Wall Street Journal*, B3.

Planning Perspectives, Inc. (2004, August 2). *Poor relationships costing US automakers*.

Poison pills. (2010, September 4). *Economist*, 65–66.

Pope, J. A., & Bartmann, D. (2010). Securing on-line transactions with biometric methods. *International Journal of Electronic Marketing & Retailing*, 3(2), 132–144.

Pope, J. A., Rau, S., Ragu-Nathan, T. S., & Ragu-Nathan, B. (2004, November). The emergence of the "chain master" in supply chain functionality. *Proceedings of the DSI Annual Meeting*, 1691–1696.

Puranam, P., & Srikanth, K. (2007, June 16–17). Seven myths about outsourcing. *Wall Street Journal*, R6.

Raffaele, P. (2007, August). The pirate hunters. *Smithsonian*, 38.

Reedy, S. (2011, February 12–13). Export shift turns rivals into allies. *Wall Street Journal*, A3.

Reiter, C., & Power, S. (2004, May 3). Volkswagen's earnings plunge 87%—first-quarter performance is hurt by weak Golf sales, adverse exchange rates. *Wall Street Journal*, A10.

Rotary International. (2011). Guiding principles. Retrieved June 18, 2011, from http://www.rotary.org/en/AboutUs/RotaryInternational/GuidingPrinciples/Pages/ridefault.aspx

Rothfield, M. (2010, December 30). Another arrest in "expert-network" probe. *Wall Street Journal*, C3.

Rowley, I., & Hiroko, T. (2009, January 19). How the strong yen has weakened Japan. *BusinessWeek*, 50.

Sanchanta, M. (2011, March 29). Chemical reaction: iPod is short key material. *Wall Street Journal*, B1.

Sanders, P. (2009a, July 2). Boeing tightens its grip on Dreamliner production. *Wall Street Journal*, B1.

Sanders, P. (2009b, December 23). Boeing takes control of plant. *Wall Street Journal*, B2.

Sauder "insourcing" parts . . . and jobs. (2010, January 1). *Toledo Business Journal*, 1.

Schoofs, M. (2007, September 21). ATMs become handy tool for laundering dirty cash. *Wall Street Journal*, A1.

Schroeder, R., Goldstein, S., & Rungtusanatham, J. (2011). *Operations management*. New York, NY: McGraw-Hill.

Schumpeter, J. (1954). *History of economic analysis*. New York, NY: Oxford University Press.

Shining a light. (2010, December 11). *Economist*, 76.

Ship stays put after alert. (2007, May 22). *International Herald Tribune (IHT)*, 7.

Slosson, M. (2011, July 1). Los Angeles firms bring apparel jobs home on cost concerns. *Reuters*. Retrieved July 8, 2011, from http://www.reuters.com/assets/print?aid=USTRE7602DT20110701

Smith, A. (1937). *An inquiry into the nature and causes of the wealth of nations*. New York, NY: Modern Library.

So much gained, so much to lose. (2009, November 7). *Economist*, 11.

Spegele, B. (2011, May 11). First solar sets joint venture in China. *Wall Street Journal*, B5.

Standage, T. (2009, September 26). Mobile marvels: A special report on telecoms in emerging markets. *Economist*, 13–19.

Stoll, P. (2005, December 5). Lear is told to supply parts to Chrysler until court hearing. *Wall Street Journal*, A6.

Swiss bank modifies detailed dress code derided for detail. (2011, January 23). *Toledo Blade*, G4.

Trent, R. J., & Roberts, L. R. (2010). *Managing global supply chain and risk*. Fort Lauderdale, FL: J. Ross Publishing, Inc.

Tsi, T-I, & Clark, D. (2009, March 6). Taiwan to shore up its struggling chip sector. *Wall Street Journal*, B1.

Vandenbosch, M., & Sapp, S. (2010, August 23). Keep your suppliers honest. *Wall Street Journal*, R8.

Vonderembse, M. A. (2002). *Improving supply chain performance: The case of Modine Manufacturing and Daimler-Chrysler*. Bedfordshire, England: The European Case Clearing House.

Wakabayashi, D. (2009, November 30). Sharp's new plant reinvents Japan manufacturing model. *Wall Street Journal*, B1.

Walker, W. (2002, March). The supply chain squeeze. *APICS Magazine*, 29.

Whitehouse, M. (2010, February 13). Radical shifts take hold in U.S. manufacturing. *Wall Street Journal*, B1.

Wild, J., Wild, K., & Han, J. (2010). *International business*. Upper Saddle River, NJ: Prentice Hall.

Williamson, E. (2011, March 4). U.S., Mexico agree to settle truck feud. *Wall Street Journal*, A1.

Williamson, O. (1998). Transaction cost economics: How it works and where it is headed. *De Economist, 146*(1), 23–58.

Williamson, O. (2009). Transaction cost economics: The natural progression. Nobel Prize lecture, December 18, 455–476.

Winchester, S. (2008, December 21). How America can maintain its edge. *Parade*, 8–10.

Winning, D., & Lee, M-J (2011, February 15). Asia bids for Australia's rich resources. *Wall Street Journal*, B3.

Wonacott, P. (2011a, January 13). A continent of new consumers beckons. *Wall Street Journal*, B1.

Wonacott, P. (2011b, June 13). Banking via a cellphone and a shack. *Wall Street Journal*, C1.

World Bank. (2010, November 4). *Doing business 2011: Making a difference for entrepreneurs*. Washington, DC: Author. Retrieved June 19, 2011, from http://www.doingbusiness.org/reports/global-reports/doing-business-2011

Worthen, B. (2007, November 27). Too many workers fail to grasp the value of data, risks of loss. *Wall Street Journal*, B3.

Zamiska, N., & Kesmodel, D. (2007, November 19). Tainted ginger's long trip from China to U.S. stores. *Wall Street Journal*, A1.

Zimmerman, A. (2010, August 11). Boom makers say BP left them adrift. *Wall Street Journal*, A3.

Zoellner, T. (2007, February 18). Is your medicine dangerous to your health? *Parade Magazine*, 4.

Glossary

APICS	American Production and Inventory Management Society, now known as the Association for Operations Management.
Benelux	Belgium, the Netherlands, and Luxembourg.
BRIC	Brazil, Russia, India, and China.
CDMA	Code division multiple access (mobile phone technology).
CPIM	Certified in Production and Inventory Management (APICS).
CPSD	Certified Professional in Supplier Diversity (ISM).
CSCP	Certified Supply Chain Professional (APICS).
ERP	Enterprise resource planning.
EU	European Union.
Eurozone	Countries in the EU that have adopted the euro (€) as a common currency.
GATT	General Agreement on Tariffs and Trade (1949–93).
GPS	Global positioning system.
GSM	Global System for Mobile Communication (mobile phone standard).
ISM	Institute for Supply Management (see PMA).
JIT	Just-in-time. The generic version of TPS.
Malcolm Baldrige Award	A competitive quality award for U.S. firms.
MRP	Material requirements planning.
MRP II	Manufacturing resource planning.
OECD	Organization for Economic Co-operation and Development.
PIGS	Portugal, Ireland, Greece, and Spain.
PMA	Purchasing Management Association, now known as the Institute for Supply Management (ISM).
PPP	Purchasing power parity. Tells what an exchange rate should be.
RFID	Radio-frequency identification.
SCM	Supply-chain management.
SCOR Model	Supply-Chain Operational Reference Model from the Supply Chain Council.
SCOR-P	SCOR Professional certification by the Supply Chain Council.

SKU	Stock-keeping unit. The basic measure of an item in the inventory stock.
TEU	Twenty-foot equivalent unit. An ocean container standard size.
TOC	Theory of constraints.
TPS	Toyota Production System, later known as JIT and lean.
WIP	Work-in-process inventory.
WTO	World Trade Organization.

Disclosures

Of the organizations and companies mentioned in this book, the author is a member of APICS and Rotary and has a financial interest in AT&T and Johnson & Johnson. The author's family has a financial interest in Citizens Bank and First Solar.

Index

The letters *f* and *t* following a page number denote a figure or table respectively.

Announcing the Business Expert Press Digital Library
Concise E-books Business Students Need for Classroom and Research

This book can also be purchased in an e-book collection by your library as
- a one-time purchase,
- that is owned forever,
- allows for simultaneous readers,
- has no restrictions on printing,
- can be downloaded as PDFs from within the library community.

Our digital library collections are a great solution to beat the rising cost of textbooks. E-books can be loaded into their course management systems or onto students' e-book readers.

The **Business Expert Press** digital libraries are very affordable, with no obligation to buy in future years.

For more information, please visit **www.businessexpertpress.com/librarians**. To set up a trial in the United States, please contact **Sheri Allen** at *sheri.allen@globalepress.com*; for all other regions, contact **Nicole Lee** at *nicole.lee@igroupnet.com*.

CPSIA information can be obtained at www.ICGtesting.com
Printed in the USA
BVOW030709120911

270870BV00007B/8/P